D1540984

A Place at the Table

Introduction

The Paige Whitney Babies Center was founded in September, 1992, by Deborah and Harold Imperatore as a memorial to their daughter, Paige Whitney, who died from Sudden Infant Death Syndrome at the age of two months. The Center's mission is to provide, free of charge, the basic necessities for babies up to two and a half years old who come from disadvantaged homes and to provide academic scholarships for all qualified parents in the program. Additionally, the Center strives to alleviate feelings of resentment that parents often develop toward their babies; deter working poor parents from resorting to welfare; preserve the relationship between parent and baby rather than turning to foster care; and reassure parents that their babies are special and deserving of love and concern.

Contributions made to the Center, without exception, are used exclusively to purchase provisions for the Center's babies or to provide academic scholarships for the parents. All parents are eligible for the Center's program regardless of where they reside, their race or religion.

The Center established an Academic Scholarship Program in 1996. It is intended to help parents to develop a sense of independent self-worth and pride; to establish goals for their lives and be conscientious about doing their best to achieve them; and to set a good example for their children by showing that education helps to improve their life.

"Essentially," says Deb Imperatore, "we're trying to create a brighter future for babies and their families."

A Place at the Table

Credits

Published by: The Paige Whitney Babies Center

Copyright© The Paige Whitney Babies Center
1 East Oak Street
Basking Ridge, New Jersey 07920

Library of Congress Catalog Number: 98-060479
ISBN: 0-9662554-0-2

Designed and Manufactured by
Favorite Recipes® Press
an imprint of

FRP™

P.O. Box 305142
Nashville, Tennessee 37230
Manufactured in the
United States of America

Book designer: Steve Newman

First Printing: 1998   7,500 copies

About the Artists

Using the theme, *A Place at the Table,* Joy
Wallis created lively watercolors representing the
variety of places where one can eat. For this
cookbook she collaborated with her friend,
Cindy Petterson, who drew the charming line
and wash illustrations.

Joy writes, "There are two sides to my art.
One is the life of its own as a picture develops
before my eyes. It is a delight. The other is the
discipline of saying, 'It's 9:00 AM, time to start
whether I want to or not.' Both are needed. It
would be lovely to look out the window and say,
'This is a painting day.' That does not happen for
me. Experience has taught me that paintings do
not come uninvited. I have
to get up in the morning
and set the table, then
art can come in and
take its place."

*The Paige Whitney Babies Center responds to
God's directive in Deuteronomy 15:11b to
"freely open your hand to your brother, to your
needy and poor in your land."*

We dedicate A Place at the Table *to
all our volunteers who give of themselves with
love and concern to improve the quality of life of babies
from disadvantaged homes and their families.*

A Place at the Table *was conceived to build public
awareness about The Paige Whitney Babies Center
and to raise funds to support the needs of
disadvantaged babies and their families.*

Contents

Foreword

From darkness there came a great light. From deep despair was born an eternal hope. This is the good news story of our Christian faith. It is the story of God being present and at work among us in Jesus Christ. It is also the story of the vital ministry and mission of The Paige Whitney Babies Center.

In August of 1991, Deborah and Harold Imperatore suffered the tragic loss of their daughter, Paige Whitney, who died from Sudden Infant Death Syndrome at the age of two months. It was an experience of immeasurable loss. It was a time of darkness and despair. Yet as God surrounded them with compassion and love, it also became an experience of deepened faith, of hope, and an opportunity for Christ's light to shine brightly. A year after their daughter's death, The Paige Whitney Babies Center was founded, with the ambitious mission of helping to care for the basic necessities of children from disadvantaged homes. Nearly two thousand families—and two million diapers—later the scope of their ministry continues to grow. It is a living testament, a shining beacon, of redemption— of God transforming hopelessness into hope and death into life.

Now, as a part of the Center's outreach comes *A Place at the Table,* a delightful book of delicious recipes, each lovingly chosen and caringly compiled. May it bring you and your loved ones meals and experiences that will nourish you in body and spirit as you gather around your own table. May it also serve as a reminder of the one holy table where we all have a place, where all of us as God's children are treated with love and dignity, with respect and compassion, and where we too can be transformed and made new.

Dennis W. Jones
Associate Pastor
The Presbyterian Church of Basking Ridge

First and Foremost

First and Foremost

Artichoke Roll

1 loaf French bread
5 T. butter
2 garlic cloves, minced
2 tsp. sesame seed
1 (7½-oz.) can artichoke bottoms, chopped
1 C. Gruyère cheese
½ C. sour cream
1 C. grated Parmesan cheese
1 tsp. lemon juice
Salt and freshly grated pepper to taste
Sprigs of fresh tarragon or parsley for
    garnish

Crumble the scooped out bread and reserve it. In a skillet sauté the garlic, sesame seed, and reserved crumbs in the butter, stirring, until the crumbs and seeds are lightly browned. Remove the pan from the heat and stir in the artichoke, ½ cup of the Gruyère, sour cream, Parmesan, lemon juice, and salt and pepper and spread the mixture in the bread shells. Sprinkle the tops with the remaining Gruyère.

Wrap each shell in foil and bake the shells in a preheated 350° F. oven for 25 minutes. Unwrap the loaves and bake them for 5 minutes more, or until the cheese begins to bubble. Let the loaves cool for 5 minutes, cut them into 1-inch slices, and arrange them on a serving plate. Garnish the plate with the tarragon or parsley.

The loaves can be frozen after they are filled and wrapped, but if using frozen rolls, the baking time should be increased by 10 to 15 minutes.

Serves 8 to 10.

Artichoke and Red Pepper Croutons

These croutons make a fine hors d'oeuvre as well as a splendid accompaniment to a soup lunch.

8 slices country-style bread, preferably homemade
$1/4$ C. extra virgin olive oil, or to taste
1 (4-oz.) jar roasted red peppers
1 (13-oz.) can artichoke bottoms, sliced
$1/2$ lb. Fontina cheese, very thinly sliced

Arrange the bread on a baking sheet and brush each slice with the oil. Arrange the peppers and artichoke bottoms on top. Top the slices with the cheese and put the croutons under a preheated broiler for 2 to 3 minutes, or until the cheese is melted. Quarter each slice.

Serves 8.

Croutons with Smoked Trout and Herbed Butter

A recipe from Chef Jim Lupia

1 loaf French or Italian bread, cut into $1/2$-inch slices
1 stick butter, softened
2 T. Italian seasoning
1 tsp. freshly ground pepper
1 lb. smoked trout fillets, peeled and sliced diagonally

Arrange the bread slices on a baking sheet and toast them in a 400° F. oven for 5 to 10 minutes, or until they are just golden. Let the toasts cool.

In a bowl combine the butter, Italian seasoning, and pepper. Spread the mixture on the toasts and top each piece with a portion of the trout.

Smoked trout can be found in sealed packages in the specialty food departments of most supermarkets.

Makes 20 to 25 toasts.

Chutney Cheddar Pennies

1 C. flour
5¹/₂ oz. extra-sharp Cheddar cheese, grated
4 T. butter
³/₄ tsp. ground ginger
Tabasco to taste
1 large egg
¹/₄ C. finely chopped mango or peach chutney

In a food processor combine the flour, cheese, butter, ginger, and Tabasco and process the mixture until it is crumbly. Add the egg and process the mixture until it forms a ball. Roll the dough into a log 1¹/₄ inches in diameter and chill it for 30 minutes in the freezer or 1 hour in the refrigerator, or until it is solid enough to slice cleanly.

Cut the log into slices about ¹/₈ inch thick, arrange them on a baking sheet, and with the thumb press an indentation into each slice. Fill the indentations with chutney and bake the hors d'oeuvres in a preheated 425° F. oven for about 12 minutes, or until they are golden brown. Transfer the hors d'oeuvres to a serving plate and serve them warm or at room temperature. The log can be frozen, well wrapped, and cut, filled, and baked at a later time.

Makes about 3 dozen hors d'oeuvres.

Since its inception, The Paige Whitney Babies Center has distributed over two million diapers. Seated side by side, two million babies would stretch from Basking Ridge, NJ to Portland, ME.

Grilled Goat Cheese Dolmades

8 (½-inch) rounds of chèvre, each about
    1½ inches in diameter
½ C. extra virgin olive oil
1 T. *herbes de Provence*
1 garlic clove, crushed
Freshly ground black pepper
8 grape leaves, rinsed if they are canned
¼ C. finely chopped walnuts, toasted
1 loaf of French bread, cut into ¾-inch
    slices and toasted lightly in the oven.

In a bowl combine the oil, *herbes*, garlic, and pepper and let the cheese marinate in the mixture for at least 2 hours.

Spread out the grape leaves and put a round of cheese in the center of each leaf. Sprinkle the cheese with the nuts. Fold the sides of each leaf over the cheese and roll up the cheese slices inside the leaves to enclose them completely. Brush the outside of each cheese "package" with the remaining marinade and on a preheated very hot grill (if the grill is not very hot, the cheese will melt and run out before the packages are cooked) grill the packages for about 2 minutes on each side. Divide the packages among four hors d'oeuvre plates and serve them warm with the toasted French bread.

Serves 4.

Olive Cheese Balls

A long-time favorite. Great to keep on hand for unexpected guests.

2 C. grated Cheddar cheese
½ C. butter, softened
1 C. sifted flour
¼ tsp. Tabasco
½ tsp. salt
1 tsp. paprika
30 to 40 small stuffed green olives, drained
    and patted dry

In a food processor combine the cheese and butter and add the flour and seasonings to form a paste. Wrap about a teaspoon of the mixture around each olive, covering it completely. On a baking sheet bake the balls at 400° F. for 15 minutes. Makes 30 to 40 hors d'oeuvres.

Alternatively, the unbaked balls may be frozen on a baking sheet until firm, packed in plastic bags, and stored in the freezer, until they are ready to use.

Serves 6 to 8.

Moroccan Eggplant

Truly delicious! A wonderful addition to a picnic supper.

1 large eggplant, unpeeled and diced
3 T. extra virgin olive oil
8 oz. tomato sauce
3 garlic cloves, minced
1 green pepper, seeded and chopped
1 T. ground cumin
1/2 tsp. cayenne pepper
2 tsp. sugar
2 tsp. salt
1/4 C. balsamic vinegar
1 T. minced fresh coriander

In a large wok or heavy skillet heat the oil. Add all the ingredients except the coriander and cook the mixture over moderate heat, covered, for 20 minutes. If the mixture still has a lot of liquid, boil it until the liquid disappears but the mixture is still moist. Chill the mixture, covered, and stir in the coriander just before serving. Serve the eggplant with toasted pita bread.

Makes about 2 cups.

In 1992, its first year, The Paige Whitney Babies Center helped fifty babies. Five years later the number had increased to four hundred and fifty.

Herbed Cheese Cherry Tomatoes

12 oz. Montrachet or other soft mild chèvre
1/4 C. heavy cream
3 T. finely snipped chives
1 tsp. thyme
1/2 tsp. freshly ground pepper
1/2 tsp. lemon juice
1 tsp. grated lemon rind
1 pt. cherry tomatoes, tops cut off
Sprigs of fresh dill

In a food processor process the cheese and slowly pour in the cream, processing the mixture until it is smooth. Scrape the mixture into a bowl and whisk in the chives, thyme, pepper, lemon juice, and lemon rind. Chill the mixture, covered with plastic wrap, for at least 3 hours. Makes about 2 cups.

Scrape the seeds and partitions out of each tomato. (If the tomatoes are large enough, a melon ball cutter works well for this process.) Salt the inside of the tomatoes and let them drain for at least 30 minutes.

Using a demitasse spoon, put some of the cheese mixture into each tomato and arrange the tomatoes on a serving plate. Garnish the tomatoes with the sprigs of dill.

Serves 6 to 8.

The tomatoes may alternatively be stuffed with one of the following stuffings:

Pesto Mayonnaise

1 C. mayonnaise
1/2 C. Fresh Basil Pesto (see page 109)
Salt and freshly ground pepper to taste

In a bowl combine the mayonnaise and pesto, add the salt and pepper, and chill the mixture, covered with plastic wrap.

Makes about 1 1/2 cups.

Anchovy and Caper Mayonnaise

1 C. mayonnaise
2 tsp. minced garlic
Pinch of salt
2 tsp. lemon juice
12 or more anchovy fillets, minced
1 T. capers, minced

In a bowl combine all the ingredients and chill the mixture, covered with plastic wrap.

Makes about 1 1/2 cups.

Portobello Mushrooms with Tomato Pesto and Pancetta

A recipe from Chef Jim Lupia

6 portobello mushrooms
Extra virgin olive oil
6 oz. tomato paste
6 oz. freshly grated Parmesan cheese
6 very thin slices pancetta or prosciutto, sautéed until crisp
6 slices smoked mozzarella cheese

Brush the mushrooms, inside and out, with the oil and in a skillet sauté them over moderately high heat for 2 to 3 minutes on each side. Transfer the mushrooms, top sides down, to a baking sheet.

In a bowl combine the tomato paste and Parmesan cheese and spread some of the mixture evenly on each mushroom. Put a slice of pancetta or prosciutto on each mushroom and top each mushroom with a thin slice of mozzarella. Broil the mushrooms for 1 to 2 minutes, or until the cheese is bubbly. The mushrooms can be served whole or cut into wedges and served with wooden picks.

Serves 6.

Happiness is like a butterfly — the more you chase it, the more it will elude you. But if you turn your attention to other things, it comes and softly sits on your shoulder.

Caramelized Leek and Sun-Dried Tomato Tart

Rich and delicious. Serve it with a salad for an elegant supper or as a first course.

2 lb. leek, trimmed and well rinsed
1 T. butter
2 T. sugar
2 oz. oil-packed sun-dried tomatoes, drained
   and chopped
1 sheet frozen puff pastry (from a 17$\frac{1}{4}$ oz.
   package)
Salt and pepper to taste

Slice the white part of the leek into 1-inch slices, discarding the green tops. In a skillet melt the butter, spread the leek in the pan in one layer, and sprinkle it with 1 tablespoon sugar and salt and pepper. Add enough cold water to barely cover the leek, bring it to a boil, and simmer the leek for 30 minutes, or until it is tender and all the liquid has evaporated to a sticky glaze.

Oil well the bottom and sides of an 8-inch tart pan and sprinkle it with the remaining 1 tablespoon sugar. Add the tomatoes and arrange the leek over the tomatoes to cover the bottom of the pan. Sprinkle the leek with salt and pepper to taste.

Roll out the pastry and cut a circle 1 inch larger than the tart pan. Arrange it over the leek, tucking the excess inside the pan, and pierce the top in several places. Bake the tart in a preheated 425° F. oven for 20 minutes, or until the pastry is crisp and golden.

Serves 6 to 8.

Texas Onion Toasts

20 thin slices of French bread from a
  baguette loaf
1/4 to 1/3 C. extra virgin olive oil
2 T. butter or margarine
2 large red onions, halved and thinly sliced
1 tsp. sugar
3 T. red-wine vinegar
1 T. honey
1/2 tsp. snipped fresh thyme, or 1/4 tsp. dried
1/4 tsp. salt
1/8 tsp. freshly ground pepper
Sprigs of fresh thyme

On a baking sheet toast the bread, 4 inches from
the broiler, for 1 minute, or until it is lightly browned,
turn the slices, and broil the other sides for 1 minute.
Brush one side of each slice lightly with the olive oil.

In a large saucepan melt the butter or margarine
and in it cook the onions, covered, over low heat, stirring
occasionally, for 15 minutes. Remove the pan from the
heat, stir in the sugar, and return the pan to moderate
heat. Cook the onions for 5 minutes more, stirring
occasionally, and stir in the vinegar, honey, snipped
thyme, salt, and pepper.

Using a slotted spoon, put about 1 tablespoon of
the onion mixture on each crouton, arrange the hors
d'oeuvres on a serving plate, and garnish the plate with
the sprigs of thyme. If desired, the toasts can be served at
room temperature.

Serves 8 to 10.

*The leek, the onion, and the
cabbage – ancient
Egyptians raised them to
the rank of gods.*

Crisp Mushroom Roll

1 lb. mushrooms, trimmed and chopped
1/2 C. minced onion
2 shallots, minced
2 T. butter
1 T. vegetable oil
1/2 C. sour cream
2 T. minced dill
Salt and freshly grated white pepper to taste
4 leaves of phyllo dough
5 T. butter, melted

Put the mushrooms in a towel, twisting the towel around them, and squeeze them to release some of the moisture. In a saucepan sauté the mushrooms with the onion and shallots in the 2 tablespoons butter and the oil, stirring frequently, until the moisture has evaporated. Stir in the sour cream, dill, and salt and pepper and let the mixture cool.

Put one of the phyllo leaves on a sheet of wax paper, keeping the remaining leaves covered with plastic wrap and a damp towel, and brush it with the melted butter. Top it with a second leaf and brush the top with butter. (Do not be alarmed if the leaves tear slightly. It is important to handle them gently and to keep them well covered so they will not dry out, but phyllo is very forgiving and a tear in one sheet will be covered by another.) Spread half the filling in a strip along one of the long sides of the buttered phyllo, fold in the edges of the phyllo to contain the filling, and roll up the phyllo sheets like a jelly roll to form a long narrow log. Brush the roll on all sides with butter, reheating the butter as necessary to keep it of brush-on consistency. Gently transfer the roll to a buttered baking sheet.

Make another roll with the remaining filling and sheets of phyllo in the same manner. (At this point the rolls may be frozen, well wrapped, for later baking.) Bake the rolls in a preheated 350° F. oven for 45 minutes, or until the pastry is deep golden and crisp. Let the rolls cool for 5 minutes and slice them into 1-inch slices. Serve the slices warm.

Serves 8 to 10.

Fresh Tomato Chutney

A delightful condiment that perks up hash browns, rice, or sandwiches.

> 2 large shallots, chopped
> 2 T. extra virgin olive oil
> 2 large tomatoes, peeled and cut into 1-inch
>   chunks
> 1 T. minced garlic
> 2 T. balsamic vinegar
> 1 T. sugar
> Salt and pepper to taste
> 2 T. minced fresh basil

In a skillet cook the shallots in the oil over moderate heat until they are golden. Add the tomatoes and garlic and cook the mixture over moderately high heat, stirring, until the tomatoes have released their juice. Stir in the vinegar, sugar, and salt and pepper and cook the mixture for 3 to 4 minutes, or until it is slightly thickened. Let the mixture cool until it is just slightly warm and stir in the basil.

Makes about 1 1/2 cups.

To make tomatoes easily "peelable," put them in a brown paper bag and set the bag in the sink. Pour boiling water into the bag and let the tomatoes stand until the bag breaks – about 20 seconds. Refrigerate the tomatoes until they're needed. The skins will slip right off.

Spinach Balls with Mustard Sauce

*The Mustard Sauce makes a piquant addition
to this long-standing favorite.*

 2 (10-oz.) packages frozen chopped spinach,
   thawed and squeezed dry
 1 C. grated Parmesan cheese
 1 stick butter, melted
 1/2 C. minced shallot
 3 large eggs
 1/2 tsp. nutmeg
 2 C. herb stuffing mix, crushed, or seasoned
   fine bread crumbs
 1/2 tsp. salt
 Pepper to taste

In a bowl combine all the ingredients, shape
the mixture into 1-inch balls, and bake the balls on
a greased baking sheet in a preheated 350° F. oven
for 20 minutes, or until they are lightly browned
and slightly crusty. Serve the balls warm with
mustard sauce.

Makes about 45 balls.

Mustard Sauce

 4 T. dry mustard
 1/2 C. sugar
 Pinch of salt
 2 large eggs, lightly beaten
 1/2 C. white vinegar
 1/2 C. half-and-half

In a saucepan combine all the ingredients and
cook the mixture, stirring, until it is thickened. Let
the sauce cool and serve it at room temperature.

Makes about 1 1/2 cups.

Chill until firm

Roasted Red Pepper Bateaux

This exceptionally pretty vegetable preparation is delicious as a first course, accompanied by toasted croutons made from thinly sliced French bread, or as a festive side dish. The peppers can be prepared several hours ahead and baked an hour before serving.

> 4 large red peppers, halved lengthwise and seeded with stems left on
> 6 tomatoes, peeled and coarsely chopped
> 8 tinned anchovy fillets, finely chopped
> 2 garlic cloves, minced
> 8 tsp. extra virgin olive oil
> Salt and freshly ground pepper
> 2 T. minced fresh basil

Arrange the peppers, cut sides up, in an oiled baking pan and divide the tomatoes among them. Divide the anchovies and garlic over the tomatoes, drizzle 1 teaspoon of the oil over each pepper half, and season the peppers with the salt and pepper. Roast the peppers on the top shelf of a preheated 350° F. oven for 50 minutes. Pour any collected juices into the peppers and sprinkle the tops with the basil. Transfer the peppers to a serving plate or to individual plates.

Serves 8.

Babies and children play with donated toys and books while their parents, waiting for their supplies from the Center, look through donated adults' and children's clothes. When the children realize they can take their newfound treasures home, their faces are a delight to see.

Fresh Plum Salsa

2 large red or black plums, pitted and diced
1 plum tomato, seeded and diced
1 large nectarine, diced
1 tsp. lemon juice
1/2 tsp. minced fresh tarragon
2 tsp. canned minced chilies (mild or hot)
    or 1/2 tsp. minced serrano chile
1/4 tsp. grated orange rind

In a glass or ceramic bowl combine all the ingredients and let the mixture macerate for at least 4 hours. Serve the salsa as an accompaniment to grilled meats, especially pork.

Makes about 3 cups.

Walnut-Stuffed Mushrooms

1/2 C. minced onion
1 1/2 T. extra virgin olive oil
1 T. butter
1 garlic clove, minced
2 1/2 T. chopped walnuts
6 oz. frozen chopped spinach, thawed and
    squeezed dry
1 1/2 oz. feta cheese, crumbled
1 oz. Gruyère cheese, grated
3 T. minced fresh dill
Salt and freshly ground white pepper to
    taste
16 medium mushroom caps

In a skillet cook the onion in the olive oil and butter over moderate heat, covered, for about 25 minutes, or until it is translucent and lightly colored. Add the garlic and walnuts and cook the mixture for 1 minute. Add the spinach and cook the mixture, stirring, for 5 minutes. Let the mixture cool slightly and stir in the cheeses, dill, and salt and pepper.

In an oiled baking dish arrange the mushroom caps hollow sides up. Divide the stuffing among them and bake them in the upper third of a preheated 400° F. oven for 8 to 10 minutes, or until the stuffing is slightly browned. Transfer the mushrooms to a serving plate and serve them warm.

Serves 4.

California-Style Guacamole

1 ripe avocado, peeled and pitted
2 T. tomato salsa (or 1 tomato, diced, mixed with
   2 T. minced onion)
1 to 2 T. minced fresh cilantro
1 T. mayonnaise
2 tsp. lemon juice
1 tsp. ground cumin
1/4 tsp. chili powder
1/4 tsp. garlic powder
Salt and pepper to taste

In a bowl mash the avocado with a potato masher, leaving some chunkiness. Add the remaining ingredients, and adjust the seasoning. Serve the guacamole with tortilla chips.

Makes about 1 cup.

Early settlers in Bernards Township needed a meetinghouse and a place of worship. Accordingly, a simple log cabin was built in the early 1700s, on the site of the present Presbyterian Church of Basking Ridge.

Crab Crostini

8 oz. lump crab meat, cartilage removed
1/2 C. finely chopped red pepper
2 T. plus 2 tsp. mayonnaise
2 T. minced fresh parsley
1 T. minced fresh chive
1 T. lime juice
1 T. Dijon-style mustard
1 T. grated Parmesan cheese
4 or 5 drops Tabasco
Salt to taste
1 loaf Italian bread, cut into 16 slices

In a bowl combine the red pepper, mayonnaise, parsley, chive, lime juice, mustard, cheese, Tabasco, and salt, blending the mixture well. Stir in the crab meat and spread 1 tablespoon of the mixture on each slice of bread. Arrange the slices in a broiler pan and broil them under a preheated broiler for 5 to 6 minutes, or until they are lightly browned. Transfer the crostini to a serving plate and serve them warm. (The crab mixture may be stored in the refrigerator, covered, for several hours before baking.)

Serves 8.

Avocado Dipping Sauce

1 large ripe avocado, peeled, seeded, and cut into chunks
3 anchovy fillets
1/4 C. shallot mustard
1 C. homemade-type mayonnaise
3 T. sour cream
1 garlic clove, minced
3 T. minced parsley
1 T. raspberry vinegar
Salt and freshly ground white pepper to taste

In a food processor combine all the ingredients and blend the mixture, scraping down the sides of the bowl as necessary, until it is smooth. Correct the seasoning and blend the mixture again. Transfer the mixture to a serving bowl and chill it, covered. Serve the sauce with crudités.

Makes about 2 cups.

Soups and Salads

Soups and Salads

Roasted Corn and Red Pepper Chowder

6 ears corn, husked
2 red peppers
1/4 lb. lean bacon, diced
2 C. chopped onion
3 T. flour
4 C. low-sodium chicken broth
2 baking potatoes, diced
1 1/2 C. half-and-half
Salt and freshly ground white pepper to
    taste
3 T. chopped scallion

On a grill cook the corn and red peppers over moderately high heat, turning frequently, for 12 to 15 minutes, or until they are slightly charred. (Or roast the corn and peppers under a broiler, turning them frequently, until they are slightly charred.) Put the peppers into a paper bag and let them stand for 10 minutes. Cut the kernels from the corn and peel, seed, and dice the peppers.

In a Dutch oven sauté the bacon until it is crisp, transfer it with a slotted spoon to paper towels to drain, and pour off some of the grease. Add the onion and sauté it until it is translucent. Stir in the flour and cook the mixture for 2 minutes. Gradually stir in the broth and bring the mixture just to a boil. Add the potatoes and cook the mixture over moderately low heat for 10 minutes. Add the corn, peppers, and half-and-half and simmer the mixture for 15 minutes. Stir in the bacon, simmer the soup for 5 minutes more, or until it is slightly thickened, and season it with the salt and pepper. Ladle the soup into bowls and garnish each serving with a bit of the scallion.

Serves 8.

Asparagus Tomato Soup

A flavorful light soup, perfect for lunch with a creative bruschetta.

3/4 lb. asparagus, cooked
1 onion, chopped
2 C. stewed tomatoes
1 carrot, chopped
2 tsp. chopped fresh parsley
1 bay leaf
1/2 tsp. thyme
1/2 tsp. basil
5 C. chicken broth
1 tsp. salt
Freshly ground pepper
2 T. butter, melted
2 T. flour

In a large saucepan combine all the ingredients except the butter and flour and simmer the mixture for 15 minutes. Transfer the mixture to a food processor, purée it, and return it to the pan. In a small dish stir the butter into the flour to make a paste and stir the paste into the purée. Cook the soup for 10 minutes, or until it is thickened.

Serves 4.

Cream of Chicken and Broccoli Soup

1/2 C. sliced mushrooms
1/2 C. chopped onion
1/2 C. butter
1/4 C. flour
2 C. evaporated skim milk
1 1/2 C. chicken broth
1/4 tsp. pepper
1 C. cubed cooked chicken
1 C. chopped broccoli
1/4 tsp. rosemary
1/2 tsp. salt
1/4 tsp. thyme

In a large saucepan sauté the mushrooms and onion in the butter until the onion is soft, add the flour, and cook the mixture, stirring, for 2 minutes. Gradually stir in the milk and broth and cook the mixture over moderate heat, stirring, until it is smooth. Add the remaining ingredients, reduce the heat to moderately low, and simmer the soup for 20 minutes. Serve this soup with pita toasts spread with an herbed butter (page 142).

Serves 3 or 4.

Creamy Eggplant Soup

An unusual soup with a delectible flavor.

1 large eggplant, peeled and cut into large chunks
2 large onions, quartered
1 green pepper, seeded and halved
1 (28-oz.) can tomatoes
2 C. milk
1 C. light cream
2 garlic cloves, minced
2 T. fresh oregano, or 1 T. dried
2 T. fresh basil, or 1 T. dried
Salt and freshly ground pepper to taste

On a greased baking sheet roast the eggplant and onions in a preheated 375° F. oven for l hour, or until they are soft. Roast the pepper, cut sides down, until the skin is dark, put it in a plastic bag for 10 minutes, and peel it. Transfer the eggplant, onions, and pepper to a food processor with the remaining ingredients and process the mixture until it is puréed but not completely smooth, adding more milk if necessary. Pour the soup into a saucepan and heat it until it is hot.

Serves 4.

Since the Center opened its doors in 1992, two sets of quadruplets, five sets of triplets, and fourteen pairs of twins have received baby goods.

Curried Leek and Carrot Soup

An easy, light soup, which can be prepared ahead.

2 C. diced carrots
2 C. diced leek
4 T. butter
3 C. chicken stock
1 tsp. curry powder, or to taste
Salt to taste
1/2 to 1 C. light cream (optional)

In a saucepan cook the carrots in lightly salted water to cover until they are tender and drain them, reserving 1 cup of the cooking water. Purée the carrots with the reserved water in a food processor or blender.

In a heavy skillet cook the leek in the butter until it is wilted and purée it in the food processor or blender with the chicken stock. In a saucepan combine the carrots and leek, add the curry and salt, and stir in the cream, if desired. Heat the soup or chill it and serve it cold. If the soup is to be served cold, let it chill for at least 24 hours before serving.

Serves 4 to 6.

Florentine Onion Soup

A recipe from Chef Jim Lupia
Rich and warming on a chilly evening.
Wonderful accompanied by Tuscan focaccia.

6 T. extra virgin olive oil
8 large yellow onions, thinly sliced
8 leeks, diced
8 scallions, white parts only, thinly sliced
5 garlic cloves, minced
1/2 lb. pancetta, cut into 1/4-inch dice
12 C. rich chicken stock (rich chicken stock can be made by using canned chicken broth: buy twice the amount called for in the recipe and cook until reduced by half)
8 T. balsamic vinegar
2 C. Chianti or Zinfandel
Salt and freshly ground pepper to taste
1/2 lb. freshly grated Parmesan cheese
1/4 C. minced fresh Italian parsley

In a large pot heat the oil, add the onions, leeks, scallions, garlic, and pancetta, and cook the vegetables for about 15 minutes, or until the onions are soft and the pancetta is light golden. Add the stock and simmer the mixture for 30 minutes. Add the vinegar, wine, and salt and pepper. Ladle the soup into bowls and top each serving with some of the cheese and parsley.

Serves 12.

Gingered Scallop Soup

This is a delicious soup, but it's not enough for a meal by itself. Add a rice salad and some crusty bread.

1½ T. minced peeled gingerroot
1 large garlic clove, minced
5 peppercorns
1 tsp. soy sauce
1 tsp. sesame oil
1½ T. dry Sherry
7 C. chicken stock or broth
½ lb. snow peas, strings removed and cut
    diagonally
1 lb. sea scallops, thinly sliced
1 (8-oz.) can sliced water chestnuts
1 C. chopped scallion
2 carrots, cut into 1-inch julienne

In a large pot combine the gingerroot, garlic, peppercorns, soy sauce, sesame oil, Sherry, and stock and bring the liquid to a boil. Add the vegetables and scallops and cook the soup for 3 minutes.

Serves 4.

When a baby is accepted into the program, the family receives a clothes basket brimming with baby necessities, plus hand-knitted items such as hats, sweaters, booties, and blankets. More than one hundred and fifty blankets have been made by one of our senior volunteers!

Zucchyssoise

1½ C. sliced leek
2 lb. zucchini, trimmed and thinly sliced
⅓ C. butter
3½ C. chicken broth
1 C. sliced cooked potatoes
1½ T. minced fresh tarragon, or 1 tsp. dried
1 C. evaporated milk
½ tsp. nutmeg
Salt and pepper to taste

In a large saucepan sauté the leek and zucchini in the butter until they are softened, add the broth, and simmer the mixture for 15 minutes. Add the potatoes, transfer
the mixture to a food processor, and purée it. Mix in the remaining ingredients and serve the soup hot or chilled.

Serves 4.

Texas Tortilla Soup

A hearty, healthy starter or, in larger portions, a meal.

2 T. butter
2 T. vegetable oil
1 large onion, chopped
1 jalapeño (optional), seeded and minced
4 garlic cloves, minced
2 large carrots, diced
6 celery ribs, diced
1 lb. cooked chicken, chopped
1 tsp. ground cumin
1 tsp. chili powder
1 tsp. salt
1 tsp. lemon pepper
1 tsp. Tabasco, or to taste
½ C. flour
1 (14-oz.) can crushed tomatoes
1½ qt. chicken broth
1 (8-oz.) package tortilla chips
1 avocado, peeled and diced
½ C. sour cream
¾ C. grated Monterey Jack cheese

In a pot heat the butter and oil and in it sauté the onion, garlic, jalapeño, carrots, and celery until the vegetables are softened. Stir in the chicken, let the mixture simmer for 5 minutes, and stir in the cumin, chili powder, salt, lemon pepper, Tabasco, and flour. Add the tomatoes and broth and let the soup simmer for 1 hour.
　　Put a few tortilla chips in the bottom of 6 to 8 soup cups, ladle in the soup, and garnish each serving with a spoonful of sour cream and a sprinkling of avocado and cheese.

Serves 6 to 8.

Sherried Squash Bisque

1 (2-lb.) Butternut squash
1 onion, finely chopped
2 T. extra virgin olive oil
1 (14½-oz.) can diced tomatoes
2 T. dry Sherry
3 C. chicken broth
⅔ C. milk
2 T. minced fresh thyme, or 2 tsp. dried
Salt and freshly ground pepper to taste
⅓ C. plain yogurt
Sprigs of fresh thyme

In a greased baking pan bake the squash in a preheated 350° F. oven for 1 hour and 10 minutes, or until it is very soft. Let the squash cool slightly, peel it, and scoop out the seeds. Cut the squash into chunks.

In a large saucepan sauté the onion in the olive oil over moderately high heat for 5 minutes. Add the squash, tomatoes, and Sherry, bring the mixture to a boil, and stir in the broth. Bring the soup to a boil, reduce the heat to moderately low, and simmer the soup, covered, stirring occasionally and breaking up the squash with the back of the spoon, for 30 minutes. Stir in the milk and thyme, continuing to break up the large chunks of squash, and return the soup to a simmer. Add the salt and pepper and ladle the soup into heated bowls. Top each serving with a dollop of yogurt and a sprig of thyme.

Serves 6.

Purée minced herbs with a little water and freeze the purée in ice cube trays, ready to be swirled into soups, sauces, or stews.

Chilled Zucchini Curry Soup

A lovely soup to look at and to taste. Its zesty flavor belies its healthful benefits.

2 lb. zucchini, trimmed and coarsely
  chopped
1 C. chopped scallion
4 T. butter
1 T. curry powder
1 T. ground cumin
2 C. chicken broth
3 C. buttermilk
Salt and freshly ground pepper to taste
$1/2$ carrot, very thinly sliced

In a large saucepan cook the zucchini and scallion in the butter, covered, over moderate heat until the zucchini is softened. Stir in the curry and cumin, cook the mixture for 2 to 3 minutes, and add the broth. Transfer the mixture to a food processor, in batches, and purée it. Pour the mixture into a large bowl or plastic container and stir in the buttermilk and salt and pepper. Chill the soup, covered, for at least 4 hours.

Stir the soup before serving and, if it is too thick, stir in water or buttermilk until it is the desired consistency. (It should be fairly thick.) Ladle the soup into bowls and garnish each serving with some of the sliced carrot.

Serves 6.

Winter Soup

All that's needed to make this an excellent meal on a cold night is a loaf of peasant bread and some olive oil for dipping.

$1^{1/2}$ oz. dried porcini mushrooms, chopped
2 T. extra virgin olive oil
1 C. chopped shallot
2 lb. potatoes, peeled, if desired, and diced
1 lb. kielbasa, halved lengthwise
$1^{1/4}$ C. lentils, rinsed, soaked, and drained
$1^{1/2}$ tsp. thyme
7 C. beef broth
Salt and freshly ground pepper to taste

In a small bowl pour 1 cup boiling water over the porcini and let the porcini stand for 20 minutes.

In a large pot heat the olive oil and in it sauté the shallot for 5 minutes, or until it is soft. Add the potatoes, kielbasa, lentils, thyme, and broth and stir in the porcini, reserving the soaking liquid. Strain the soaking liquid into the pot, discarding any sediment, and cook the soup, stirring occasionally, for 1 hour and 15 minutes, or until the lentils are tender and the soup is thick.

Transfer the kielbasa to a cutting board and slice it. Transfer $1^{1/2}$ cups of the soup to a food processor or blender and purée it. Return the kielbasa and purée to the pot and stir in the salt and pepper.

Serves 6.

Glorious Raspberry Green Salad

4 C. mixed salad greens, light and dark colors,
    mild and sharp flavors
Almond Raspberry Vinaigrette
¹/₂ C. sliced almonds, toasted
¹/₂ C. raspberries

In a large bowl toss the greens with Almond Raspberry Vinaigrette and sprinkle the salad with the almonds and raspberries. Toss the salad gently.

Serves 4.

Almond Raspberry Vinaigrette

¹/₂ C. vegetable oil
¹/₄ tsp. grated lemon rind
3 T. lemon juice
2 T. ground toasted almonds
1 tsp. Dijon mustard
2 T. seedless raspberry jam
Pinch of salt

In a bowl combine all the ingredients and whisk the mixture until it is smooth.

Makes about 1 cup.

Make a living wreath for the center of the table by setting a wet florist's foam wreath on a large plate and inserting sprigs of green herbs.

Creamy Apple and Endive Salad

½ C. heavy cream
3 T. red-wine vinegar
4 large Granny Smith apples, peeled, cored,
    and thinly sliced
1 head curly endive, stems discarded and
    leaves torn into pieces
½ C. crumbled Gorgonzola cheese
Salt and freshly ground pepper

In a large bowl combine the cream and vinegar and add the apples. Add the endive and cheese, toss the salad to combine it well, and add the salt and pepper.

Serves 8.

Mango Salad

3 C. mesclun
1 very ripe mango, peeled and chopped
2 oz. Feta cheese, crumbled
½ red pepper, roasted and cut into strips
Parsley sprigs
Balsamic vinegar or Vinaigrette Dressing

In a salad bowl layer the mesclun, mango, and cheese, and garnish the salad with the red pepper and parsley. Sprinkle the top with the balsamic vinegar or Vinaigrette Dressing.

Serves 4.

Vinaigrette Dressing

2 T. white-wine vinegar or lemon juice
½ tsp. Dijon mustard
Salt and pepper to taste
⅓ C. extra virgin olive oil
1 T. mixed fresh minced herbs, such as
    parsley, chives, or tarragon
1 garlic clove, crushed

In a bowl whisk together the vinegar, mustard, and salt and pepper. Whisk in the oil, a little at a time, and continue to whisk the dressing until it is well blended. Stir in the herbs and garlic.

Makes about ½ cup.

Chicken, Peach, and Wild Rice Salad

4 chicken breast halves, poached with the bone
    in, cooled, skinned, and cubed
3 C. cooked wild rice
1 C. Peach Vinaigrette
3/4 C. sliced almonds, toasted
1 C. sliced celery
Salt and freshly ground pepper to taste
2 C. cubed peeled peaches
2 tsp. lemon juice
1 head Bibb or Boston lettuce

In a large bowl combine the chicken and rice
and toss the mixture with Peach Vinaigrette. Fold in the
almonds and celery and add the salt and pepper. In
a bowl toss the peaches with the lemon juice and fold
them into the salad, reserving about 1/4 cup for garnish.
Arrange the lettuce leaves on a platter, mound the salad
inside them, and sprinkle the reserved peaches on top.

Serves 6.

Peach Vinaigrette

1/2 C. vegetable oil
1/4 C. extra virgin olive oil
1/4 C. tarragon or raspberry vinegar
1/2 peeled peach
1/8 tsp. cayenne
1/2 tsp. salt
Freshly ground white pepper to taste

In a blender or food processor combine all the
ingredients and blend the dressing until it is almost
smooth.

Makes about 1 cup.

When only a teaspoon or so of lemon juice is needed, pierce a lemon with a skewer and squeeze.

Blue Cheese, Chicken, and Almond Salad

1 lb. chicken breast, cooked and diced
1/2 lb. fresh spinach, tough stems discarded
1 small red onion, thinly sliced
1 red pepper, seeded and cut into julienne
2 oz. sliced almonds, toasted
Salt and pepper to taste

In a bowl combine all the ingredients and toss the mixture with Blue Cheese Dressing to taste.

Serves 4.

Blue Cheese Dressing

1/2 C. balsamic vinegar
1/4 C. honey
1 tsp. Dijon mustard
1 C. vegetable oil
1/2 C. crumbled blue cheese
Salt and pepper to taste

In a bowl whisk together the vinegar, honey, and mustard and add the oil in a thin stream, whisking. Stir in the blue cheese and season the dressing with salt and pepper.

Makes about 2 cups.

Pear, Blue Cheese, and Walnut Salad

2 large heads Boston lettuce
2 large firm Bosc pears, cored and chopped
3/4 C. crumbled blue cheese
3/4 C. chopped walnuts
Vinaigrette Dressing (page 40)

In a large bowl toss the lettuce, pears, blue cheese, and walnuts and dress the salad with Vinaigrette Dressing to taste.

Serves 10 to 12.

Southwest Orzo and Bean Salad

A pleasant variation on traditional bean salad, tastefully enlivened by the chili peppers.

3 C. cooked orzo
1 (19-oz.) can kidney beans, drained and rinsed
1 (19-oz.) can black beans, drained and rinsed
1¼ C. frozen peas, thawed
1 C. sliced celery
1 (4½-oz.) can chopped mild green chili peppers
2/3 C. chopped red onion
¼ C. chopped coriander
Salt and pepper to taste
1/3 C. red-wine vinegar
¼ C. water
1 tsp. minced garlic
½ tsp. salt
Pepper to taste
¼ C. vegetable oil

In a large bowl combine the orzo, beans, peas, celery, chili peppers, onion, and coriander. Season to taste with salt and pepper. In another bowl combine the vinegar, water, garlic, salt, and pepper and gradually whisk in the oil. Pour the dressing over the orzo mixture, tossing, and chill the salad, covered, for at least 4 hours.

Serves 8 to 10.

Eating is not merely a material pleasure. Eating well gives a spectacular joy to life and contributes immensely to goodwill and happy companionship. It is of great importance to the morale.

Elsa Schiaparelli (1890–1973), Italian fashion designer

Korean Layer Salad

1 lb. orzo
2 T. sesame oil
5 carrots, shredded in a food processor
2 C. white raisins
2 C. sunflower seeds
1/3 C. finely chopped scallion
3 T. minced parsley plus additional parsley
    for garnish

In a large saucepan cook the orzo according to the package directions, drain it, and rinse it in cold water. Toss the orzo with the sesame oil and transfer half of it to a glass bowl. Top it with half of each of the remaining ingredients, except the parsley garnish, and repeat the process. Pour the Sesame Oil Dressing over the salad and sprinkle the top with the remaining parsley.

Serve the salad immediately or chill it, covered, and serve it the following day. It should be tossed before serving if it is kept overnight.

Serves 12.

Sesame Oil Dressing

3/4 C. corn oil
1/2 C. rice vinegar
1/4 C. sesame oil
Pinch of salt
1 T. sugar
2 T. grated orange or lemon rind
1 tsp. pepper
1 tsp. minced peeled gingerroot
1 tsp. soy sauce
1 garlic clove, minced
1/2 tsp. dried red pepper

In a bowl whisk together all the ingredients.

Makes about 1 1/2 cups.

Chicken Sesame Salad

A summer dinner salad – take this along to concerts in the park.

6 oz. pecans, chopped
2 tsp. butter
$^1/_2$ tsp. salt, or to taste
$^1/_2$ tsp. rosemary
1$^1/_2$ lb. boneless skinless chicken breasts, cooked and cut into $^1/_2$-inch dice
1$^1/_3$ C. rice, cooked and cooled
12 cherry tomatoes, halved
1 large avocado, cut into $^1/_2$-inch dice
Chick-Pea Dressing

Spread the pecans on a small baking sheet, dot them with the butter, and sprinkle them with the salt and rosemary. Toast the pecans, tossing them once or twice with a fork, until they are deep brown and let them cool.

In a large bowl combine the chicken, rice, pecans, tomatoes, and avocado and toss the mixture with the dressing.

Serves 6.

Chick-Pea Dressing

1$^1/_2$ C. canned chick-peas
2 garlic cloves
$^1/_3$ C. rice vinegar
2 T. soy sauce
$^1/_4$ C. sesame oil
$^1/_4$ C. vegetable oil

In a blender or food processor purée the first 4 ingredients and with the machine running pour in the oils.

Music that fills the air with glee comes not from man but from a lovely old tree. Harmonious and sweet are the melodies performed by the birds – and the concert is free!

Curried Tomato and Pasta Salad

An excellent salad: Ordinary ingredients produce an extraordinary result.

8 oz. cooked pasta twists (about 2¹/₂ C. uncooked)
1 C. chopped yellow pepper
1 lb. fully ripe tomatoes, cut into ¹/₂-inch dice (about 2)
¹/₂ C. halved and thinly sliced zucchini
2 T. cider vinegar
1¹/₂ tsp. curry powder
1 tsp. sugar
¹/₂ tsp. minced garlic
¹/₄ tsp. salt
Freshly ground pepper
¹/₂ C. vegetable oil

In a large bowl combine the pasta, pepper, tomatoes, and zucchini. In a bowl combine the vinegar, curry, sugar, garlic, salt, and pepper and whisk in the oil. Pour the dressing over the pasta mixture to taste, combining it well, and chill the salad, covered, for several hours before serving.

Serves 6 to 8.

Pasta and Chicken Summer Salad

1 lb. cheese ravioli or tortellini, cooked and cooled
1 C. cubed cooked chicken
¹/₂ C. snow peas, ends, strings removed, and very lightly blanched
¹/₂ C. whole seedless red grapes
¹/₂ C. diced artichoke bottoms (about 3)
¹/₂ C. mayonnaise
¹/₂ C. cucumber slices
¹/₄ C. celery
¹/₄ C. sliced scallion
2 kiwis, peeled and sliced
2 mandarin oranges, sectioned
Salt and pepper to taste

In a large bowl combine all the ingredients, toss the salad gently, and chill it. Add the salt and pepper to taste.

Serves 4 to 6.

Summer Dinner Salad

1/2 to 3/4 head Napa cabbage, shredded
1 bunch scallions, trimmed and chopped
1 1/2 lb. cooked boneless skinless chicken breast,
    cut into 1-inch chunks
2 packages Ramen Noodle Soup mix
3/4 C. slivered almonds
3 T. sesame seed
2 T. sugar
1/4 C. rice wine vinegar
1/2 C. peanut oil
2 T. soy sauce
1 flavor packet from noodle mix
1 tsp. sesame oil

In a large bowl combine the cabbage, scallions, and chicken. With a rolling pin or heavy bottle gently crush the noodles while they are still wrapped, being careful not to break the package. On a baking sheet toast the almonds, the evenly crumbled noodles, and sesame seed until they are lightly browned and let them cool.

In a saucepan combine the sugar, vinegar, peanut oil, soy sauce, and contents of the flavor packet. Simmer the mixture for 1 minute, stir in the sesame oil, and let the mixture cool.

Add the almond mixture and the sugar mixture to the vegetables and combine the salad well. For ease of preparation, the various mixtures can be prepared early in the day and assembled just before serving.

Serves 6.

After a good dinner one can forgive anybody, even one's own relations.

Oscar Wilde (1854–1900)

Few things give more people more pleasure than food.

Broccoli Salad

1 large bunch uncooked broccoli, cut into
    small pieces
1 small red onion, chopped
1 C. shredded Cheddar cheese
1/2 lb. bacon, cooked crisp and crumbled
1 (8-oz.) can sliced water chestnuts, drained

In a large bowl combine all the ingredients and
toss them with Mayonnaise Dressing.

Serves 6.

Mayonnaise Dressing

2/3 C. mayonnaise
1/4 C. cider vinegar
Salt and pepper to taste

In a bowl whisk the mixture until it is smooth.

Jicama, Mango, and Watercress Salad

*Peeling and cutting the mangoes can be a bit of
a challenge, but the finished product is definitely
worth the effort.*

3/4 C. walnut oil or extra virgin olive oil
6 T. white-wine vinegar
5 T. chopped fresh cilantro
3 T. plus 1/2 C. chopped toasted pecans
Salt and freshly ground pepper to taste
2 large bunches watercress, trimmed
2 C. 2-inch-long matchstick-size strips
    peeled jicama
2 C. 2-inch-long matchstick-size strips
    peeled mango
2 small red peppers, cut into 2-inch-long
    matchstick-size strips

In a small bowl whisk together the oil, vinegar,
and cilantro, stir in the 3 tablespoons pecans, and
season the dressing with salt and pepper. In a large
bowl combine the watercress, jicama, mango, and
peppers, toss the salad with the dressing, and
correct the seasoning. Divide the salad among eight
plates and sprinkle it with the remaining pecans.

Serves 8.

Picnic Salad

The peppery taste of arugula makes this salad a fine complement to grilled steak.

2³/4 C. fresh corn kernels, or frozen kernels,
    thawed and drained
1 pint cherry tomatoes, halved
4 celery stalks, chopped
¹/2 red onion, chopped
¹/2 lb. arugula, stems trimmed and leaves torn
    into bite-size pieces
2 T. balsamic vinegar
¹/3 C. extra virgin olive oil
Salt and freshly ground pepper
1 C. crumbled blue cheese (about 4 oz.)

In a large bowl combine the first 5 ingredients. In a small bowl gradually whisk the oil into the vinegar and season the mixture with salt and pepper. Add ³/4 cup cheese and the dressing, and toss the salad. Sprinkle the remaining cheese over the salad. The salad can be prepared up to 4 hours in advance and kept covered and chilled.

Serves 6 to 8.

A man hath no better thing under the sun, than to eat, and to drink, and to be merry.

Ecclesiastes 8:15

New Potato and Green Bean Salad

Add a pound of cooked kielbasa to make this salad a delectable main course.

1/4 C. balsamic vinegar
2 T. lemon juice
2 T. Dijon mustard
1 garlic clove, minced
Dash of Worcestershire sauce
1/2 C. extra virgin olive oil
Salt and pepper to taste
1 1/2 lb. small red potatoes
3/4 lb. small green beans, trimmed
1 small red onion, coarsely chopped
1/4 C. chopped fresh basil

In a bowl whisk together the vinegar, lemon juice, mustard, garlic, and Worcestershire sauce and gradually whisk in the oil. Season the dressing with salt and pepper.

In a vegetable steamer steam the potatoes until they are tender, let them cool, and quarter them. In a pot of boiling salted water cook the beans for 2 to 3 minutes, or until they are crisp-tender, drain them, and transfer them to a bowl of ice water. Drain the beans and halve them. In a large bowl combine the potatoes, beans, onion, and basil and add the dressing to taste, tossing the salad. Season the salad with salt and pepper and serve it at room temperature.

Serves 6 to 8.

Sunshine Salad with Honey Cumin Dressing

6 T. extra virgin olive oil
3 T. balsamic vinegar
1 1/2 tsp. honey
3/4 tsp. ground cumin
3/4 tsp. chili powder
Salt and freshly ground pepper to taste
1 large bunch watercress, trimmed
1 head Boston lettuce, torn into bite-size pieces
1/2 red onion, thinly sliced
2 oranges, peeled and sliced crosswise

In a small bowl whisk together the oil, vinegar, honey, cumin, and chili powder and season the dressing with salt and pepper. In a large bowl combine the watercress, lettuce, onion, and orange, toss the mixture with the dressing, and correct the seasoning.

Serves 4 to 6.

Tuscan Bread Salad

A recipe from Chef Jim Lupia

    4 C. cubed day-old country bread (about 8 oz.)
    2 lb. tomatoes, cored, seeded, and coarsely
        chopped
    1 red onion, diced
    ½ cucumber, peeled, seeded, and cubed
    2 celery heart ribs, cubed
    ½ C. loosely packed basil leaves, coarsely
        chopped
    4 large garlic cloves, minced
    1 C. drained pitted green olives (about 5 oz.),
        halved crosswise
    1 egg yolk
    3 T. red-wine vinegar
    1 T. balsamic vinegar
    2 anchovy fillets
    6 T. extra virgin olive oil
    Salt and freshly ground pepper to taste

In a large bowl combine the bread, tomatoes, onion, cucumber, celery, basil, garlic, and olives and toss the mixture. In a blender or food processor blend the egg yolk, vinegars, anchovy, and olive oil until the mixture is smooth. Add the salt and pepper to taste. Pour the dressing over the salad, toss the salad, and let it stand for at least 30 minutes before serving in order to allow the bread to absorb the dressing.

Serves 4 to 6.

There are hundreds of languages in the world, but a smile speaks all of them.

Vermilion Salad

An unusual and memorable salad. Served in a clear glass bowl, it is also beautiful on the table.

1 small head red cabbage (about 1½ lb.),
    cored and cut into wedges
Ice water
⅔ C. safflower oil
⅓ C. raspberry vinegar
1 T. honey
1 tsp. salt
1 tsp. cinnamon
Freshly ground pepper
2 small beets, peeled
2 large unpeeled pears, halved and cored
⅔ C. chopped walnuts

Arrange the cabbage in the feed tube of a food processor and slice it thin, using firm pressure. Transfer it to a large bowl, add enough ice water to cover it, and let it soak for 30 minutes. Drain the cabbage well and return it to the bowl.

In the food processor combine the oil, vinegar, honey, salt, cinnamon, and pepper, blend the mixture for 3 seconds, and let it remain in the work bowl. Arrange the beets in the feed tube and shred them. Arrange the pears in the feed tube and shred them. Add the mixture to the cabbage and toss it well. (The salad can be prepared to this point one day in advance of serving and chilled, covered.)

Before serving, drain any liquid, add the walnuts, and adjust the seasoning.

Serves 4 to 6.

Balsamic Vinaigrette

3 T. balsamic vinegar
1 T. Dijon-style mustard
Salt and pepper to taste
1 C. extra virgin olive oil

In a bowl whisk together the vinegar, mustard, and salt and pepper. Dribble in the olive oil in a slow stream, whisking constantly, until the dressing is creamy and thickened and the oil has been incorporated. Correct the seasoning.

Makes about 1¼ cups.

Shredded Vegetable Salad

1 C. shredded daikon
1 C. shredded bok choy
1 C. shredded carrot
1 C. shredded romaine
1/3 C. coarsely chopped peanuts
Sesame Soy Dressing

In a salad bowl combine all the ingredients and toss the mixture with Sesame Soy Dressing.

Serves 4 or 5.

Sesame Soy Dressing

1/4 C. sesame oil
1/3 C. rice-wine vinegar
1/2 tsp. sugar
2 T. soy sauce

In a small bowl whisk together all the ingredients until the dressing is well blended.

Makes about 2/3 cup.

The area which now constitutes Bernards Township lay under the Wisconsin glacier 12,000 years ago. The Great Swamp is actually the remains of a post-glacial lake. Both mammoth and mastodon skeletons have been found in New Jersey.

Basil Dressing

½ C. chopped fresh basil
1 C. mayonnaise
½ C. sour cream
½ C. minced fresh parsley
3 scallions, chopped
2 T. vinegar
1 tsp. Worcestershire sauce
2 T. minced fresh chives
1 garlic clove, minced
½ tsp. dry mustard
Freshly ground pepper to taste

In a bowl combine all the ingredients until the dressing is well blended.

Makes about 2 cups.

Creamy Herb Dressing

Fresh herbs are the secret to the great flavor of this dressing.

⅓ C. minced fresh parsley
¼ C. chopped scallion
1 C. sour cream
¼ C. mayonnaise
½ C. buttermilk
1 tsp. minced fresh thyme
¼ tsp. salt
¼ tsp. freshly ground pepper

In a small bowl combine all the ingredients until the mixture is smooth. Chill the dressing, covered, for at least 1 hour before serving.

Makes about 2 cups.

Entrées

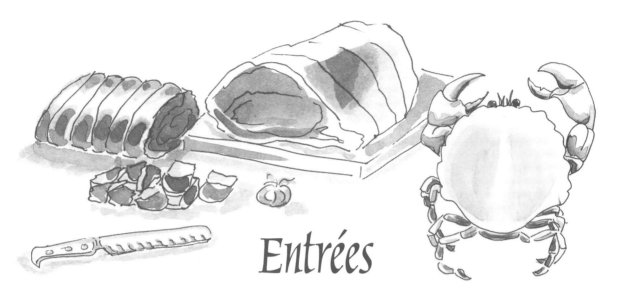

Entrées

Spicy Cumin Tomato Beef Ragout

1 (3-lb.) beef bottom round, trimmed and
    cut into 1- by 2-inch pieces
1/2 C. vegetable or canola oil
4 large onions, chopped
5 T. minced peeled gingerroot
3 large garlic cloves, minced
2 T. ground coriander
1 T. paprika
2 tsp. turmeric
1/2 tsp. red pepper flakes
1 lb. new potatoes
1 (28-oz.) can crushed Italian tomatoes
1/2 C. chopped fresh coriander
1 T. cumin seed
Salt to taste

In a bowl toss the meat with 2 tablespoons of the oil, coating it evenly. In a large skillet heat 2 tablespoons oil over high heat and in it brown the meat on all sides, in two batches, for about 4 minutes for each batch. Transfer the meat to a 5-quart casserole.

Add the remaining 4 tablespoons oil to the skillet and in it cook the onions for 15 to 20 minutes, or until they are browned. Stir in the ginger and garlic and cook the mixture for 1 minute. Stir in the ground coriander, paprika, turmeric, and red pepper, add the potatoes, and cook the mixture for 4 minutes. Add the tomatoes and 3 cups boiling water, combine the mixture well, and pour it over the meat. Bake the casserole, covered tightly, in a preheated 325° F. oven for 2 hours, or until the meat is very tender. Turn off the oven and let the meat stand in the oven for 15 minutes more.

In a small skillet roast the cumin seed over moderately high heat, shaking the pan constantly, for 2 minutes, or until it is browned, and transfer it to a mortar or cutting board. Crush the seed with a pestle or rolling pin and stir it into the casserole with the salt and all but 1 tablespoon of the chopped coriander. Sprinkle the remaining coriander on top.

Serves 8.

Oven-Barbecued Brisket

4-lb. beef brisket
1 onion, chopped
1 T. oil
2 T. cider vinegar
2 T. Worcestershire sauce
1 (12-oz.) bottle chili sauce
3 T. red currant jelly
1/4 C. water
3/4 tsp. salt, or to taste
6 carrots, sliced
2 T. butter or margarine

In a large pot bring the beef to a boil in water to cover over high heat, reduce the heat to low, and simmer the beef, covered, for 2 1/2 hours, or until it is tender. In a saucepan cook the onion in the oil over moderate heat until it is softened, stir in the vinegar, Worcestershire sauce, chili sauce, jelly, water, and 1/2 teaspoon salt, and bring the mixture to a boil. Let the sauce simmer over low heat for 10 minutes.

Transfer the brisket, reserving the cooking liquid, to a baking dish, spread it with half the sauce, and bake it in a preheated 450° F. oven for 15 minutes, or until the sauce is thick.

Cook the carrots in the reserved cooking liquid over low heat, covered, for 15 minutes, or until they are tender, drain them, and toss them with the butter and remaining salt.

Transfer the brisket to a cutting board, slice it thinly across the grain, and serve it with the carrots and remaining sauce.

Serves 10.

Roast Beef Tenderloin with Walnut Feta Stuffing

Absolutely prima company fare.

1 2-lb. whole beef tenderloin
1/2 C. crumbled Feta cheese
2 T. finely chopped walnuts
2 T. minced fresh parsley
2 tsp. oregano
Salt and pepper to taste
2/3 C. beef broth
Sprigs of parsley

Starting 1/2 inch from one end, cut lengthwise through the beef to within 1/2 inch of the bottom to form a long pocket. In a small bowl combine the cheese, walnuts, parsley, and 1 teaspoon oregano and spoon the mixture evenly into the pocket. Press the beef together over the stuffing and tie it at each end and in the middle with kitchen string.

Rub the remaining oregano over the tenderloin and sprinkle it with the salt and pepper. In a 13- by 9- by 2-inch flameproof baking pan roast the beef in a preheated 425° F. oven for about 30 minutes, or until a thermometer inserted in the center of the meat (not the stuffing) registers 135° F. (for medium rare). Let the meat stand at room temperature for 5 minutes and transfer it to a cutting board.

Add the broth to the baking pan and bring it to a boil over moderately high heat, scraping up the browned bits that cling to the pan. Pour the gravy into a serving dish. Slice the beef, arrange it on a heated platter, and garnish it with the parsley sprigs.

Serves 4 to 6.

Grilled Marinated Flank Steak

A well-seasoned main dish, wonderful to serve on the terrace on a summer's eve.

- ¹/₂ C. soy sauce
- ¹/₂ C. dry white wine
- ¹/₂ onion, chopped
- 3 T. minced fresh rosemary, or 1¹/₂ T. dried
- 2 T. extra virgin olive oil
- 2 garlic cloves, minced
- 1 2-lb. flank steak, trimmed
- ¹/₂ C. sour cream
- 1 T. plus 1 tsp. prepared horseradish
- 2 scallions, chopped
- Freshly ground pepper

In a glass baking dish combine the soy sauce, wine, onion, rosemary, oil, and garlic, add the steak, and let it marinate, covered, turning it occasionally, overnight.

In a small bowl combine the sour cream, horseradish, and scallions and season the sauce generously with the pepper.

Drain the marinade into a small saucepan and boil it for 1 minute. Season the steak with pepper and grill it, basting occasionally with the marinade, for about 6 minutes on each side (for rare meat). Transfer the steak to a platter and let it stand for at least 15 minutes, or up to 2 hours. Slice the steak across the grain into thin diagonal slices and serve it warm or at room temperature with the sauce.

Serves 6.

The monies needed to run The Paige Whitney Babies Center come from a variety of fundraisers, gifts from individuals and corporations, and a donation from the church in which it is housed.

Rib-Eyes Sautéed with Mustard Sauce

Melts in your mouth.

> 6 trimmed boneless rib-eye steaks, each
>   weighing about 6 oz.
> Salt and freshly ground black pepper
> 2 T. extra virgin olive oil
> 2 garlic cloves, minced
> 1/2 C. dry red wine
> 1/3 C. beef broth
> 1 T. Dijon-style mustard
> 4 T. butter, sliced
> 2 T. minced flat-leafed parsley

Rub both sides of each steak with salt and pepper and in each of two large heavy skillets heat 1 tablespoon of olive oil over moderately high heat. Cook the steaks in the pans for 3 to 4 minutes on each side (for medium rare meat) and transfer them to a platter. Cover them lightly with foil to keep them warm.

Sauté half the garlic in each skillet for about 30 seconds, divide the wine between the skillets, and reduce it by half, stirring and scraping up any brown bits. Pour the wine mixture from one skillet into the other skillet and whisk in the broth and mustard. Boil the sauce for about 2 minutes, or until it is slightly thickened, and remove the pan from the heat. Whisk in the butter, 1 piece at a time, until it is melted and add salt and pepper to taste. Pour the sauce around the steaks and sprinkle the steaks with the parsley.

Serves 6.

Creamed Meatballs with Dill

These unusual meatballs can be made smaller and served as an hors d'oeuvre.

> 2 slices white bread, crusts removed
> 3/4 C. whole milk
> 3/4 lb. ground veal
> 3/4 lb. ground beef
> 1 large egg, lightly beaten
> 1 onion, minced
> 1 tsp. salt
> 4 tsp. minced fresh dill
> Freshly ground pepper to taste
> 1 T. butter
> 1 T. vegetable oil
> 1 C. beef broth
> 1 C. light cream

In a large bowl soak the bread in 1/2 cup milk until most of the liquid is absorbed and add the veal, beef, egg, onion, salt, 2 teaspoons dill, and pepper. Combine the mixture well and blend in 3 to 4 additional tablespoons of milk, if necessary, to bind the mixture. Form the mixture into 1 1/2-inch balls.

In a large skillet brown the balls in the butter and oil. Add the broth and simmer the mixture over moderately low heat, covered, for 30 minutes. Transfer the balls with a slotted spoon to a platter and keep them warm. Add the remaining dill to the skillet and reduce the liquid by half. Pour in the cream and simmer the sauce for about 5 minutes, or until it is slightly thickened, correct the seasoning, and pour the sauce over the meatballs.

Serves 4 to 6.

Rosemary Marinated Butterflied Leg of Lamb

The wonderful part about this recipe, aside from great flavor, is being able to do most of the work a day or two beforehand.

1 (7-lb.) leg of lamb, boned and butterflied
3 C. dry red wine
1/3 C. extra virgin olive oil
2 onions, sliced
2 garlic cloves, slivered
2 1/2 T. minced fresh rosemary, or 1 1/2 T. dried
3 sprigs of parsley
2 bay leaves, crumbled
1 tsp. pepper
Sprigs of fresh rosemary for garnish

Pound the lamb until it is of approximately even thickness. In a bowl combine all the ingredients except the lamb and garnish. Put the lamb in a large heavy plastic bag and pour the marinade over it. Seal the bag, turn it several times to coat the lamb with the marinade, and let the lamb marinate, chilled, for at least 1 and up to 2 days, turning the bag occasionally.

Drain the lamb and put it on a preheated grill about 3 inches from the heat. Grill it for about 12 minutes on each side for medium rare meat. Increase the cooking time if more fully cooked lamb is desired. Transfer the lamb to a cutting board and let it stand for 10 minutes. Slice the lamb diagonally and arrange the slices on a heated platter. Garnish the platter with the sprigs of rosemary.

Serves 10.

At the holiday season, hundreds of Love Bundles are dropped off at the Center for distribution, one for each baby. A Love Bundle is comprised of enough diapers, wipes, and baby cosmetics to last five weeks, plus toilet articles for each baby's family.

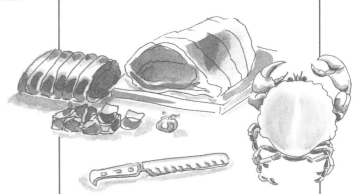

Nut-Crusted Lamb Chops

1 C. slivered almonds
1 C. shelled pistachios
1/2 C. seasoned dry bread crumbs
Salt and pepper to taste
1 C. flour
2 large eggs
1 tsp. milk
8 loin lamb chops, each 1 to 1 1/2 inches
    thick
2 T. extra virgin olive oil

In a food processor grind the nuts until they are finely chopped and transfer them to a bowl. Add the bread crumbs and salt and pepper. Put the flour on a sheet of wax paper and in another bowl whisk together the eggs and milk. Dip the lamb chops in the flour to coat them on both sides and shake off the excess. Dip them in the egg mixture and then in the nut mixture, coating them completely and lightly pressing in the nut mixture. Chill the lamb chops for at least 15 minutes.

In an overproof skillet heat the olive oil and in it brown the chops on both sides, cooking for a total of about 4 minutes. Finish cooking the chops in a preheated 425° F. oven for about 12 minutes (for medium rare meat) and transfer them to a platter.

Serves 4.

Greek Lamb Stew

A delicious mélange – great do-ahead company fare or a treat for family dinner.

1 1/4 C. minced parsley
1 (6-oz.) can tomato paste
1/2 C. dry white wine
1/4 C. red-wine vinegar
1 tsp. cinnamon
1 tsp. ground cumin
1 tsp. oregano
1/2 tsp. sugar
Salt and pepper to taste
3 lb. lean boneless lamb, cut into 1 1/2-inch
    cubes
2 lb. small white onions
2 small bay leaves
1 C. chopped walnuts
6 oz. Feta cheese, crumbled

In a large bowl combine all the ingredients except the walnuts, cheese, and tablespoon minced parsley.

Stir the mixture well to coat the meat completely. Transfer the mixture to a casserole or Dutch oven and bake it in a preheated 325° F. oven, covered, for 2 hours, or until the lamb is very tender. Sprinkle the stew with the walnuts, cheese, and reserved parsley and serve it with orzo or rice.

Serves 6.

Lamb Curry

1¹/₂ lb. trimmed boneless lamb shoulder, cut into
    1¹/₂-inch cubes
3 T. extra virgin olive oil
2 carrots, chopped
1 onion, chopped
1 T. curry powder
Pinch of cayenne
2 C. chicken broth
Salt and freshly ground pepper to taste
¹/₂ head cauliflower, separated into flowerets
³/₄ lb. green beans, trimmed
1 Granny Smith apple, peeled, cored, and
    chopped

In a large nonstick skillet brown the lamb in the oil in three batches for about 3 minutes for each batch and transfer it to a plate. Add the carrots and onion to the skillet and cook them over moderate heat for 5 minutes, or until they are browned. Add any lamb juices from the plate, the curry, and cayenne and cook the mixture, stirring, for 3 minutes. Stir in the broth and lamb and simmer the mixture for 45 minutes, or until the lamb is tender. Season the mixture with the salt and pepper.

In a saucepan of boiling salted water cook the cauliflower and beans for 4 to 5 minutes, or until they are just tender, and drain them.

Stir the apple into the lamb mixture, simmer the mixture for 10 minutes, and transfer the lamb with a slotted spoon to a large serving bowl. Pour the vegetable mixture into a food processor and purée it. Pour the purée over the lamb and arrange the cauliflower and green beans around it.

Serves 6.

Local youth groups have donated many hours on service projects for the Center. A Girl Scout troop made fifty-five baby quilts, and one Boy Scout, as part of his Eagle Badge service, raised funds and collected gifts that he gave to each family for Christmas.

Pork Tenderloin with Mustard Wine Sauce

1/2 C. vegetable oil
1/4 C. dry white wine
2 garlic cloves, crushed
1/2 tsp. thyme
1 1/2 lb. pork tenderloin
Sprigs of watercress for garnish

In a small bowl whisk together the oil, wine, garlic, and thyme and pour the mixture into a heavy plastic bag. Add the pork, seal the bag, and let the pork marinate, turning it several times, overnight.

Drain the pork, discarding the marinade, and on a preheated grill cook the pork, turning it several times, for about 25 minutes, or until a meat thermometer registers 155° F. (for meat that is just cooked through). Transfer the pork to a cutting board and let it stand for 10 minutes. Cut the pork diagonally into 1/2-inch slices and serve it with Mustard Wine Sauce. Garnish the platter with sprigs of watercress, if desired.

Serves 4 to 6.

Mustard Wine Sauce

3/4 C. dry white wine
1 T. minced shallot
3/4 C. heavy cream
2 T. Dijon mustard
Salt and freshly ground white pepper to taste

In a small saucepan combine the wine and shallot and cook the mixture over moderately high heat until the wine is reduced to about 3 tablespoons. Reduce the heat, stir in the cream, and bring the sauce to a boil. Simmer the sauce for about 3 minutes. Strain the sauce into a small bowl, discarding the shallot, and whisk in the mustard and salt and pepper.

Pork Loin Stuffed with Pine Nuts and Parsley

1 (4-lb.) boneless pork loin
Salt and pepper
1½ C. minced fresh parsley
1 C. pine nuts, lightly toasted
⅔ C. coarse grain mustard

With a sharp knife make a lengthwise cut down the side and about halfway through the loin. Open the meat and sprinkle it with the salt and pepper.

In a small bowl combine the parsley, nuts, and mustard and spread the mixture inside the pork, leaving a 1-inch border on one long side. Roll up the pork, starting from the side opposite the border and tie it at 2-inch intervals with kitchen string. Roast the pork seam side up on a rack in a roasting pan, covered loosely with foil, in a preheated 350° F. oven for 30 minutes. Turn the loin seam side down and roast it, uncovered, for 45 to 60 minutes more, or until a meat thermometer registers 165° F. Let the loin stand, loosely covered, for 15 minutes. Remove the string and slice the roast into ½-inch slices.

Serves 8.

"Full up to dolly's wax" is an old expression meaning absolutely stuffed. It comes from the day when dolls were made of wood with a head of wax — thus, the expression would have meant, full to the neck.

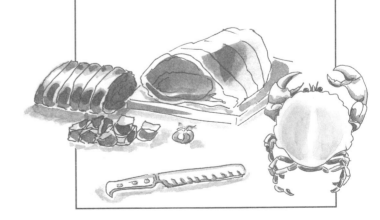

Pork Chops with Onions and Gouda Cheese

4 large (1-inch-thick) center-cut pork chops
Salt and pepper
2 tsp. paprika
2½ T. flour plus flour for dredging
4 T. vegetable oil
2 large onions, sliced
½ tsp. sugar
2 garlic cloves, minced
2 C. canned beef broth
½ C. grated Gouda cheese
1½ T. butter

Sprinkle the pork chops with the salt, pepper, and 1 teaspoon paprika and dredge them in flour, shaking off the excess.

In a large skillet brown the chops in 2 tablespoons of the oil over high heat, cooking them for about 3 minutes on each side, and transfer them to a baking dish. Add the remaining oil to the skillet and in it sauté the onions, sprinkled with the sugar, over moderately high heat, stirring frequently, for about 15 minutes, or until they are well browned. Add the garlic, sauté the mixture for 1 minute, and stir in the remaining paprika. Spoon the onions over the pork and pour in enough broth to almost cover the chops. Bake the chops, covered with foil, in a preheated 350° F. oven for 45 minutes.

Carefully pour off the cooking liquid and reserve it. With a spatula invert the chops in the baking dish so that the onions are on the bottom. Sprinkle the cheese over the chops and keep the dish warm, covered with foil, in a 200° F. oven.

In a saucepan melt the butter, whisk in the 2½ tablespoons flour, and cook the *roux*, whisking, for 3 to 4 minutes. Whisk in the reserved cooking liquid, a little at a time, bring the mixture to a boil, whisking, and cook it for 5 minutes. Season the sauce with the salt and pepper. Transfer the chops to a platter and spoon the sauce around it.

Serves 4.

Apple-Cornbread Stuffed Pork Chops

This recipe was a big hit with our testers.

4 (¹/₂-inch-thick) boneless pork loin chops, trimmed
1 tsp. thyme
Salt and pepper to taste
1¹/₂ T. butter or margarine
¹/₂ C. chopped onion
¹/₂ C. chopped peeled tart apple, such as Granny Smith
³/₄ C. cornbread stuffing mix, crushed
¹/₄ C. water

Season the pork with ¹/₂ teaspoon thyme and the salt and pepper. In a skillet melt ¹/₂ tablespoon butter and in it sauté the pork chops for about 3 minutes on each side, or until they are cooked through. Transfer the pork chops to a small baking pan.

In the skillet sauté the onion and apple in the remaining butter for about 5 minutes, or until they are softened, and stir in the stuffing mix, water, and remaining thyme. Cook the mixture, stirring, for about 30 seconds, or until the water is absorbed, and mound one-fourth of it on each pork chop. Bake the chops in a preheated 450° F. oven for about 5 minutes, or until the stuffing is crisp and beginning to brown.

Serves 2.

Fresh herbal arrangements are a lovely way to decorate a dinner table. Their fragrance awakens the senses, while their flowers and leaves provide color. A spray of parsley, mint, marjoram, or thyme beside each place setting looks especially attractive.

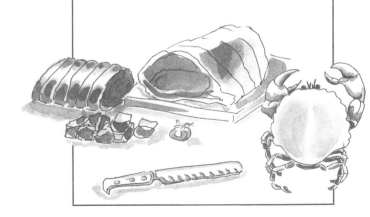

Chicken with Vegetables and Peanuts

Don't let the absence of one, or even two, ingredients (with the exception of the chicken, romaine, or peanuts) stop you from making this dish. It's an entire meal in a pot.

1 (3-lb.) frying chicken, cut into serving
    pieces, or 2 lb. skinless chicken breasts
1/3 C. peanut oil
6 T. butter
2 onions, sliced
1/2 C. diced carrot
1 red pepper, seeded and sliced
1 green pepper, seeded and sliced
1/4 C. diced celery
1 tsp. rosemary
1 tsp. basil
8 to 10 spinach leaves, coarse stems
    removed
1 garlic clove, slivered
3/4 C. sliced mushrooms
1/2 C. chopped pitted black olives
1 (6-oz.) can tomato paste
2/3 C. chicken broth
1 1/2 C. coarsely chopped romaine lettuce
Salt and pepper to taste
1/2 C. chopped peanuts
1 T. minced fresh parsley

In a large Dutch oven heat the peanut oil and in it sauté the chicken until it is lightly browned. Transfer it with tongs to paper towels to drain. Discard any oil remaining in the pan.

Melt the butter in the pan and in it cook the onions, carrot, peppers, celery, rosemary, and basil over moderate heat, stirring several times, for about 5 minutes, or until the vegetables are just tender. Add the spinach, garlic, mushrooms, and olives and cook the mixture for 2 minutes. In a small bowl combine the tomato paste with the broth and pour the mixture over the vegetables. Bring the mixture to a boil and cook it over moderate heat for 2 minutes.

Scrape the vegetable mixture into a bowl. Spread the romaine on the bottom of the Dutch oven, arrange the chicken on top of the romaine, and spoon the vegetable mixture over the chicken. Bake the chicken, covered, in a preheated 375° F. oven for 35 to 40 minutes, or until it is tender. Season the dish with the salt and pepper, sprinkle the peanuts and parsley on top, and serve the chicken and vegetables from the pan.

Serves 4 to 6.

Mexican Fajitas

1 lb. lean boneless chicken or pork, sliced into
  strips
2 garlic cloves, minced
1 onion, chopped
1 small green pepper, seeded and sliced into
  strips
1 small red pepper, seeded and sliced into strips
1 tsp. oregano
1/2 tsp. ground cumin
2 T. orange juice
Tabasco to taste
1 T. vegetable oil
Flour tortillas
Sour cream

In a bowl let the meat marinate with the garlic,
onion, peppers, oregano, cumin, orange juice, and
Tabasco for at least 30 minutes.

In a skillet heat the oil until it is hot and in it stir-fry
the meat with the marinade for 5 minutes, or until the
meat is cooked. Serve the mixture with warmed flour
tortillas and sour cream.

Serves 3 or 4.

*One cannot think well,
love well, sleep well,
if one has not dined well.*

Virginia Woolf (1882–1941),
British novelist

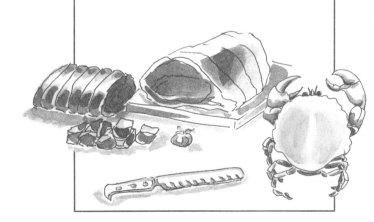

Chicken Parisienne

This unusual combination of ingredients produces an equally unusual and wonderful sauce, and the substitution of yogurt for most of the sour cream, which was in the original recipe, renders it relatively low in fat.

4 boneless skinless chicken breast halves
1/3 C. plus 1 T. flour
Salt and pepper to taste
2 T. butter
3 T. dry Sherry
1/2 tsp. tomato paste
1/2 C. chicken broth
1/2 C. low-fat yogurt
2 tsp. cornstarch
2 T. sour cream
1 T. grated Parmesan cheese
1 T. currant jelly

On a sheet of wax paper mix the 1/3 cup flour with salt and pepper and turn the chicken in the mixture to coat it, shaking off the excess. In a skillet sauté the chicken in the butter for 10 to 15 minutes, depending on the thickness of the breasts, or until it is browned on both sides and just cooked. Transfer the chicken to a plate.

In a dish or measuring cup stir the cornstarch into the yogurt, combining the mixture well. Add it to the skillet with the Sherry, 1 tablespoon flour, tomato paste, broth, sour cream, cheese, and jelly and stir the mixture over moderately low heat until the jelly is melted and the sauce is slightly thickened. Add salt and pepper to taste, if necessary. Return the chicken to the pan and cook it for 3 to 5 minutes more, or until it is heated through. Transfer the chicken to a platter and pour the sauce around it.

Alternatively, the chicken may be sautéed until it is just browned, 2 or 3 minutes on each side, and transferred to a shallow baking dish. The sauce can then be made, poured over the chicken, and the dish can then be baked in a preheated 350° F. oven for about 30 minutes. This method is excellent for the cook who is entertaining and wants to eliminate most of the work well before serving time.

Serves 4.

Chicken Breasts Espagnol

This outstanding recipe can easily be doubled, and it's terrific paired with Couscous with Almonds and Apricots (page 119).

1¼ to 1½ lb. boneless skinless chicken breasts
⅔ C. chopped pitted prunes
½ C. dry white wine
¼ C. extra virgin olive oil
¼ C. red-wine vinegar
¼ C. dark brown sugar
3 T. drained capers
1½ T. oregano
Salt and freshly ground pepper to taste
3 T. minced fresh cilantro

Arrange the chicken in one layer in an oiled baking pan. In a bowl combine the prunes, wine, olive oil, vinegar, 2 tablespoons sugar, capers, oregano, and salt and pepper and pour the mixture evenly over the chicken. Let the chicken marinate for at least 6 hours, or overnight. Sprinkle the chicken with the remaining sugar and bake it in a preheated 350° F. oven, basting it several times, for about 50 minutes, or until it is very tender. Transfer the chicken and prunes to a platter, spoon some of the juices over it, and sprinkle it with the cilantro. Pour the remaining juices into a sauceboat and pass them separately.

Serves 3 or 4.

Unfortunately many Americans live on the outskirts of hope – some because of their poverty, some because of their color, and all too many because of both. Our task is to help replace their despair with opportunity.

Lyndon B. Johnson
(1908–1973),
First State of the Union Message,
January 8, 1964

Chicken Confit with Peppers and Onions

A recipe from Chef Jim Lupia

4 boneless skinless whole chicken breasts,
    split lengthwise
Italian seasoning to taste
6 T. extra virgin olive oil
1 lb. red peppers, julienned
2 large onions, finely chopped
8 plum tomatoes, seeded and diced
3 large garlic cloves, minced
2 tsp. sugar
1/4 C. balsamic vinegar
1/4 C. tomato paste
Freshly grated Parmesan cheese to taste

Sprinkle the chicken generously on both sides with the Italian seasoning. In a large skillet sauté the chicken in 4 tablespoons olive oil over moderately high heat until it is lightly browned on both sides. Remove the chicken from the pan and reserve it.

Add the remaining olive oil to the pan and in it sauté the peppers and onions until they begin to soften. Add the garlic, sauté the mixture for 2 to 3 minutes, and add the tomatoes. Sauté the mixture for 2 to 3 minutes and add the sugar, vinegar, and tomato paste.

Spoon the mixture into a glass baking dish, arrange the chicken on top, and sprinkle it with the cheese. Bake the dish, covered with foil, in a preheated 350° F. oven for 30 minutes, transfer the chicken to a platter, and spoon the pepper mixture over it.

Serves 6.

Stir-Fried Chicken with Broccoli

1 T. soy sauce
1 T. cornstarch
5 T. peanut or vegetable oil
3/4 tsp. sugar
1 T. dry Sherry
1 large boneless skinless whole chicken
    breast, cut into bite-size strips
2 1/2 to 3 C. broccoli flowerets (about 14 oz.)
1 T. minced peeled gingerroot
1 garlic clove, minced
1 tsp. salt
1/3 C. slivered almonds, toasted

In a bowl combine the soy sauce, cornstarch, 1 tablespoon oil, 1/4 tsp. sugar, and Sherry. Add the chicken, stirring to coat it with the marinade, and let it marinate for at least 30 minutes, or, covered and chilled, up to 8 hours.

In a wok or large skillet heat 2 tablespoons oil, swirling the pan to coat it with the oil, and in it stir-fry the chicken with the marinade for about 1 1/2 minutes, or until the chicken turns white. Transfer the chicken to a plate. Add the remaining oil to the pan and in it cook the ginger and garlic for about 1 minute. Add the broccoli, stir-fry it for 1 minute, and stir in the salt, 1/4 cup water, and the remaining sugar. Cook the mixture, covered, for about 1 minute more, or until the broccoli is crisp-tender, stir in the chicken, and heat the mixture until the chicken is hot.

Serves 4.

Southwest White Chili

A new twist on the time-honored chili – though much lighter and lower in cholesterol.

½ C. chopped onion
1½ T. extra virgin olive oil
3 C. chicken broth
1 (4-oz.) can chopped green chilies, mild or hot,
    to taste
1 garlic clove, minced
1 tsp. ground cumin
½ tsp. oregano
½ tsp. cilantro
¼ tsp. ground red pepper
1¼ lb. boneless skinless chicken breasts, cooked
    and shredded
2 (19-oz.) cans cannellini, undrained
Shredded Monterey Jack cheese for garnish
Scallion slices for garnish

In a large saucepan sauté the onion in the olive oil until it is softened. Stir in the broth, chilies, garlic, cumin, oregano, cilantro, and pepper and simmer the mixture for 15 minutes. Stir in the chicken and beans, simmer the chili for 10 minutes, and serve it garnished generously with the cheese and scallion.

Serves 4.

When you hear the toast, "Here's mud in your eye," it refers to the sediment that was once frequently found in the bottom of a wine glass.

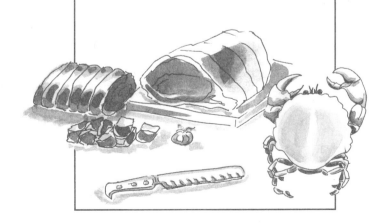

Ground Turkey Curry

Small bowls of shredded coconut, chopped fresh coriander, or chopped apple may be used as accompaniments, if desired. Children especially love this dish.

1 large onion, chopped
1½ T. butter
1½ T. curry powder
1¼ lb. lean ground turkey
1 (10¾-oz.) can cream of celery soup
⅔ cup white raisins
⅔ cup slivered almonds, lightly toasted
Salt and pepper to taste

In a large skillet sauté the onion in the butter over moderately high heat until it is golden and stir in the curry powder. Cook the onion and curry over low heat for about 5 minutes and add the turkey, breaking it up with a fork. Sauté the turkey over moderately high heat for about 8 minutes, or until it is no longer pink, and stir in the soup and 1 soup can of water. Reduce the heat to moderately low and simmer the mixture for 10 minutes. Stir in the raisins, almonds, and salt and pepper and cook the mixture for 5 minutes. Serve the curry with rice.

Serves 4.

Lime-Glazed Cornish Hens

The hens can be stuffed, if desired. A stuffing made piquant with chopped apple or cranberry or the zest of lime or orange is particularly good.

6 Cornish game hens
Salt and pepper
¼ C. butter, melted and cooled
3 T. brown sugar
3 T. lime juice
3 T. dry white wine
3 T. soy sauce
1 lime, sliced

Season the hens inside with the salt and pepper. In a small bowl combine the butter, sugar, lime juice, wine, and soy sauce and brush the hens with the sauce. Arrange the hens in a large baking pan and bake them, covered with foil, in a preheated 325° F. oven, basting every 15 minutes, for 45 minutes. Remove the foil, increase the heat to 350° F., and roast the hens, basting twice, for 10 minutes more, or until the leg joints move freely and the juices run clear when tested with a skewer. Transfer the hens to a platter and garnish them with the lime slices.

Serves 6.

Stuffed Baked Snapper

4 scallions, sliced
2 small celery stalks, chopped
6 T. butter or margarine, melted
3/4 C. fresh bread crumbs, toasted
2/3 C. chopped peeled shrimp (about 6 oz.)
2/3 C. dry white wine
1 1/2 T. minced fresh parsley
1/2 tsp. basil
1/2 tsp. thyme
1/4 tsp. salt
Pepper to taste
1 (3- to 4-lb.) whole red snapper, or 3 to 4 lb.
    snapper fillets
1/4 C. water
1/2 C. chopped onion

In a skillet sauté the scallions and celery in the butter until they are tender. Stir in the bread crumbs, shrimp, 3 tablespoons wine, parsley, basil, thyme, salt, and pepper. Stuff the mixture into the fish, or spoon it onto half the fillets and top it with the remaining halves flesh sides down. Arrange the fish in an oiled baking pan.

In a bowl combine the remaining wine, water, and onion and pour the mixture over the fish. Bake the fish, covered with foil, in a preheated 350° F. oven for 30 minutes. Remove the foil, turn the fish over, and continue to bake the fish for 5 minutes more, or until it is done.

Serves 6 to 8.

An excess of parsley may be dried – still retaining its fresh color – by microwaving it at high power for 4 minutes.

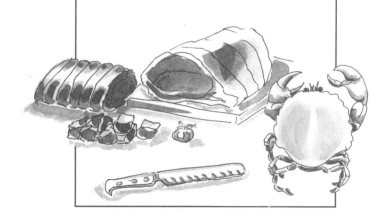

Horseradish Crusted Cod with Crispy Leek

A recipe from Simon Pearce Restaurant

4 (6-oz.) cod fillets
Seasoned flour to coat the cod
2 C. fresh bread crumbs
1/2 C. chopped shallot
4 T. unsalted butter
2 T. flour
1/2 C. dry white wine
1/2 C. aged balsamic vinegar
1/2 C. fish or chicken stock or broth
Salt and pepper to taste
3/4 C. vegetable oil, for frying
2 C. finely julienned leek, well drained
　　after washing

Make Herb Mashed Potatoes (page 98) and keep them warm.

Make Horseradish Spread.

Roll the fillets in the seasoned flour, dip them in the Horseradish Spread, and roll them in the bread crumbs, pressing the crumbs in lightly.

In a saucepan cook the shallot in 2 tablespoons butter over moderately high heat until it is golden brown. Add the 2 tablespoons flour and cook the mixture, stirring, for 5 minutes. Vigorously whisk in the wine, vinegar, and stock and reduce the mixture over moderate heat, whisking, until it is thickened to the desired consistency. Whisk in the remaining butter, add the salt and pepper, and keep the sauce warm.

In a large sauté pan heat 1/2 cup oil until it is hot but not smoking. Add the fillets and sauté them until they are golden brown on both sides. Reduce the heat to low and cook the fillets for about 5 minutes more.

In a smaller sauté pan fry the leek in the remaining oil, heated to 325° F., until it is golden and crispy. Drain the leek well and sprinkle it with salt.

Ladle about 1/4 cup of the wine sauce onto each of four plates. Put a scoop of Herb Mashed Potatoes in the center, top it with the cod and then the leek.

Serves 4.

Horseradish Spread

1 C. homemade or Hellman's mayonnaise
1/2 C. prepared horseradish
1 T. minced fresh dill
Salt and pepper to taste

In a bowl combine all the ingredients.

presentation.

aste

In a small bowl combine the first 4 ingredients. Spread the mixture on the salmon, so both sides are coated. Arrange the salmon in a buttered baking dish, and bake it in a preheated 350° F. oven for 25 minutes. Sprinkle the salmon with the paprika and parsley.

Serves 4.

Dill has long been a traditional accompaniment to poached salmon and pickles — probably because it was thought to dispel the odor of fish and render cucumbers more digestible.

Halibut with White Beans, Orzo, and Porcini

4 tomatoes
6 garlic cloves, unpeeled
2 oz. dried porcini mushrooms
1/2 C. uncooked orzo
2 C. canned small white beans, well rinsed
    and drained
6 T. extra virgin olive oil
1 1/2 T. white-wine vinegar
1/2 C. minced mixed fresh herbs, such as
    parsley, rosemary, thyme, or basil
Salt and pepper to taste
4 halibut fillets, each weighing about 6 oz.

In a baking pan roast the tomatoes and garlic in a preheated 400° F. oven for about 15 minutes for the garlic, or until it is softened, and for about 30 minutes for the tomatoes, or until the skin blisters. Press the garlic from the skins and mash it. Peel and chop the tomatoes, and in a bowl stir the mashed garlic into the tomatoes.

In a small bowl pour boiling water over the porcini and let them soften for 30 minutes. Drain and chop them.

In a saucepan cook the orzo according to the package directions and drain it. Stir in the beans, tomato mixture, and porcini and heat the mixture over moderately low heat. In a small bowl whisk together 3 tablespoons olive oil and 1 tablespoon vinegar and pour the mixture into the bean mixture. Stir in the herbs, reserving 1 tablespoon, and the salt and pepper and let the mixture cool.

Sprinkle the fillets with salt and pepper. In a skillet heat 2 tablespoons olive oil over moderately high heat and in it sauté the fillets for about 3 minutes on each side, or until they are just cooked through, and remove the pan from the heat. Divide the bean mixture among four plates and arrange the fish on the beans. Sprinkle each fillet with a bit of olive oil and vinegar and the reserved herb mixture.

Serves 4.

Sesame Glazed Salmon

A delicious, easy recipe that is equally good made with tuna.

1 C. soy sauce
1 T. cornstarch
1 T. sesame oil
1 T. minced peeled gingerroot
1 T. dry Sherry
2 tsp. honey
1/2 tsp. Tabasco
Freshly ground pepper
1 tsp. minced garlic
4 salmon steaks, each about 1 inch thick
1 bunch scallions, chopped
Additional scallions for garnish

In a food processor or blender purée the soy sauce, cornstarch, sesame oil, gingerroot, Sherry, honey, Tabasco, pepper, and garlic. Arrange the salmon in an oiled shallow baking dish, sprinkle it with the chopped scallions, and pour about two thirds of the purée over it. Bake the fish in a preheated 400° F. oven, basting it frequently with the remaining purée, for about 20 minutes, or until it is just cooked through. Transfer the salmon to a serving plate, pour any remaining purée over it, and garnish it with the scallions.

Serves 4.

Let the food be its own decoration. For a summer buffet, mold a large rice salad on a colorful plate, surround it with cherry tomatoes and basil leaves and place a sunflower on top.

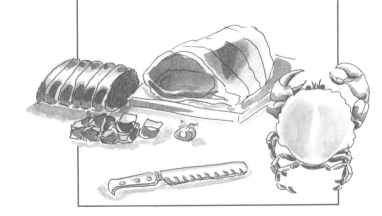

Grilled Swordfish with Pepper Corn Salsa

A colorful summery presentation.

⅓ C. lemon juice
⅓ C. extra virgin olive oil
1 tsp. ground cumin
Tabasco, salt, and freshly ground pepper to
    taste
4 swordfish steaks

In a shallow dish combine the lemon juice, olive oil, and seasonings, add the steaks, and coat them with the marinade. Let the steaks marinate for at least 1 hour.

Grill the steaks over high heat for about 2 minutes on each side, or until they are just done, and serve them with Pepper Corn Salsa.

Serves 4.

Pepper Corn Salsa

1 green pepper, seeded and diced
1 red pepper, seeded and diced
1 red onion, diced
¼ C. extra virgin olive oil
Freshly cut corn from 2 ears of corn
¾ tsp. ground cumin
Salt and pepper to taste
1½ T. lemon juice

In a saucepan sauté the peppers and onion in 3 tablespoons olive oil, stirring, for about 2 minutes. Add the corn, cumin, and salt and pepper and sauté the mixture for 2 minutes, being careful not to overcook it. The vegetables should still be slightly crisp.

Transfer the mixture to a bowl and stir in the remaining tablespoon olive oil and the lemon juice. Serve the salsa warm or at room temperature.

Makes about 2 cups.

Sole Papillote

1½ lb. sole fillets
2 C. very thinly sliced leek
¼ C. dry white wine
4 T. extra virgin olive oil
Fresh winter savory, or other fresh herb, minced
Salt and pepper to taste
4 T. butter, melted

Place one portion of sole off-center on a sheet of parchment paper and top it with ½ cup of the leek. Drizzle over it 1 tablespoon each of wine and olive oil and sprinkle it with some of the minced herb and salt and pepper. Brush the edges of the parchment with butter and fold the larger side of the paper over the fish. Fold in the ends and fold the long edges of the paper into two or three folds to enclose the fish tightly. Repeat the process with the remaining three portions of fish. Brush all four packets with butter, transfer them to a baking sheet, and bake them in a preheated 350° F. oven for 12 to 15 minutes.

Serves 4.

In ancient Rome, Aurelius was purported to have cautioned Flavius: "Take care, take care above all things that the markets of Rome be well supplied: nothing more gay or peaceful than the people when they are well fed."

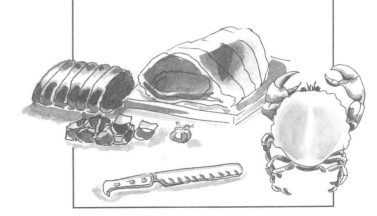

Sole with Bananas and Almonds

1/3 C. flour
Salt, pepper, and paprika to taste
6 sole fillets, halved
3 T. butter
1/2 C. dry white wine
1/4 C. honey
1 T. lemon juice
1/2 tsp. ground ginger
6 small bananas, halved lengthwise
1/2 C. sliced almonds, toasted

On a large plate combine the flour, salt, pepper, and paprika and coat the fillets in the mixture. Melt 1 tablespoon butter on a foil-lined jelly-roll pan in a 350° F. oven. Lay half the fillets on the foil, top them with the bananas, and arrange the remaining fillets over the bananas.

In a skillet melt the remaining 2 tablespoons butter over moderately low heat, stir in the wine, honey, lemon juice, and ginger, and cook the mixture, stirring, for 1 minute, or until it is hot and well combined. Pour the mixture over the fillets and bake the fish in a preheated 350° F. oven for 15 minutes. Sprinkle the dish with the almonds.

Serves 6.

Orange Grilled Swordfish

1/4 C. orange juice
1/4 C. soy sauce
2 T. catsup
2 T. vegetable oil
2 T. minced fresh parsley
1 T. lemon juice
1 garlic clove, crushed
1/2 tsp. oregano
1/4 tsp. pepper
4 swordfish steaks

In a bowl combine all the ingredients except the steaks. Pour the mixture into a large sealable plastic bag and put in the swordfish. Let the steaks marinate, turning them once, for at least 30 minutes.

On a grill broil the steaks over high heat, basting occasionally with the marinade and turning them once, for about 4 minutes on each side, depending on their thickness, or until they are just done.

Serves 4.

Gingered Tuna

3 T. minced peeled gingerroot
¹⁄₃ C. finely chopped scallion
¹⁄₃ C. soy sauce
¹⁄₃ C. rice wine or dry Sherry
1 T. sesame oil
4 large tuna steaks, about 8 oz. each
Minced fresh cilantro

In a blender purée the gingerroot, scallion, soy sauce, wine, and sesame oil. Pour the purée into a large sealable plastic bag, add the steaks, and seal the bag. Let the steaks marinate overnight, turning them once.

Remove the steaks from the marinade, reserving the marinade.

Grill the steaks over ash-white coals, or over a preheated very hot grill, basting twice with the marinade, for 5 to 8 minutes on each side, depending on the thickness. (If grilling is inconvenient, the steaks can be cooked in an oiled, shallow baking pan in a preheated 400° F. oven for about 15 minutes.) Transfer the steaks to a platter and garnish them with the cilantro.

Serves 4.

When a fellow was said to be "in need of parsley," he was at death's door — and it was believed that only parsley could save him.

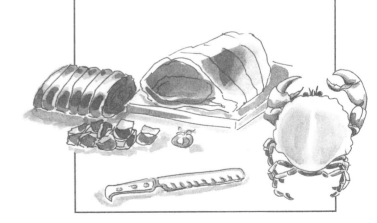

Orange Curried Shrimp

A visual knockout. Assemble all the ingredients before starting to cook.

1 mango, peeled and diced
1/2 red pepper, minced
1 tsp. sugar
4 tsp. lime juice
1 1/2 lb. shrimp, shelled and deveined
3 T. extra virgin olive oil
2 shallots, minced
2 garlic cloves, minced
1 T. minced peeled gingerroot
2 1/2 tsp. curry powder
5 T. orange juice concentrate
1 1/4 C. chicken broth
1/4 C. heavy cream
Salt and pepper to taste
2 T. minced fresh coriander

In a bowl combine the mango, red pepper, sugar, and 2 teaspoons lime juice and let the mixture macerate for 30 minutes.

In a large skillet sauté the shrimp in 2 table-spoons olive oil until they turn pink and transfer them to a plate. Add the shallots to the pan and cook them over moderately high heat until they are softened and stir in the garlic, gingerroot, and curry. Cook the mixture for 2 minutes, stir in the orange concentrate, and cook the mixture for 1 minute. Add the broth and reduce the mixture by half. Stir in the cream and cook the sauce, stirring, for about 1 minute more, or until it is syrupy.

Return the shrimp to the pan with the remaining lime juice and salt and pepper and let the mixture simmer until the shrimp are heated through. Transfer the shrimp to a platter, top them with half the mango mixture, and sprinkle the top with the coriander. Pass the remaining mango mixture separately and serve the dish with rice.

Serves 4.

Cajun Shrimp

3 slices bacon, diced
1 stick butter or margarine
2 T. Dijon mustard
1½ tsp. chili powder
½ tsp. basil
½ tsp. thyme
1 tsp. coarsely ground pepper
½ tsp., oregano
2 garlic cloves, minced
2 T. crab boil (found in the spice section of most
    supermarkets)
½ tsp. Tabasco
1½ lb. large shrimp, unshelled or shelled,
    according to taste

In a skillet sauté the bacon until it is crisp. Add the remaining ingredients, except the shrimp, and cook the mixture over moderately low heat for 5 minutes. Spread the shrimp in a flat baking dish, pour the bacon mixture over them, stirring, and bake the shrimp in a preheated 375° F. oven for 10 minutes. Stir the shrimp and bake them for 10 minutes more.

Serves 4 or 5.

Bernardston Township was so-named by the patent of 1760, issued by George II of Great Britain, in honor of Francis Bernard, Esq., his captain general and governor in the New Jersey province.

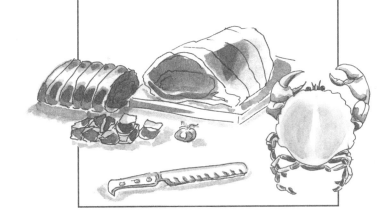

Spicy Oriental Shrimp with Peanut Sauce

½ C. canned "lite" coconut milk (found in
    the foreign foods section of most
    supermarkets)
2 garlic cloves
2 T. lime juice
1½ T. minced peeled gingerroot
2 tsp. soy sauce
2 tsp. basil
1 tsp. brown sugar
1½ lb. large shrimp, shelled and deveined,
    if desired

In a food processor combine all the ingredients except the shrimp, blend the mixture until it is smooth, and scrape it into a heavy plastic bag. Add the shrimp, close the bag, and turn it gently to coat the shrimp completely with the marinade. Chill the shrimp for at least 2 hours.

Thread the shrimp onto skewers and grill them over moderately high heat, basting once with the marinade, for about 2 minutes on each side, or until they are done. Transfer the shrimp to a platter and serve them with Peanut Sauce.

Serves 4.

Peanut Sauce

1 garlic clove
1 scallion
3 T. cold water
2 T. creamy peanut butter
2 T. sesame oil
1 T. soy sauce
1 T. red-wine vinegar
2 tsp. sugar
1 tsp. hot chili oil

In a food processor combine the garlic and scallion and chop them coarsely. Add the remaining ingredients and process the sauce, turning the machine on and off, until it is blended but not completely smooth.

Shrimp with Asparagus and Sesame Seed

Quick to prepare — and don't count on leftovers!

- 1 T. sesame seed
- 3 T. extra virgin olive oil
- 1½ lb. asparagus, trimmed and cut into 2-inch pieces
- 3 scallions, sliced
- 1½ lb. shrimp, peeled and deveined
- 4 tsp. soy sauce
- ½ tsp. salt

In a wok or a heavy skillet toast the sesame seed until it is golden, transfer it to a dish, and reserve it.

In the wok or skillet heat the oil over moderately high heat until it is hot and in it stir-fry the asparagus and scallions for 1 minute. Add the shrimp and stir-fry the mixture for about 2 minutes, or until the shrimp is no longer translucent. Stir in the soy sauce, salt, and reserved sesame seed.

Serves 4.

Bernards Township residents of the 1700s were primarily independent farmers, but as demands for goods and services increased, a water-powered mill to grind grain was built, as well as a blacksmith shop, a harness and carriage maker's shop, and several stores.

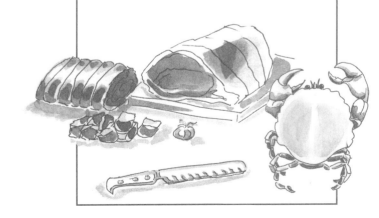

Shrimp Bahia with Rice

3 T. vegetable oil
1 onion, peeled and finely chopped
6 small tomatoes, chopped
1/4 C. minced parsley
2 lb. shrimp, peeled and deveined
1/2 tsp. pepper
Salt to taste
1 T. butter
1 T. flour
1 C. coconut milk (found in the foreign
    foods section of many supermarkets, or
    made by simmering equal amounts of
    grated unsweetened coconut and milk
    for 30 minutes and straining the milk)
1/4 tsp. crushed red pepper, or to taste

In a skillet sauté the onion in the oil until it is softened. Add the tomatoes and parsley and sauté the mixture for 5 minutes. Add the shrimp and cook the mixture, stirring constantly, for 3 minutes. Add the pepper and salt to taste.

In a small saucepan melt the butter, stir in the flour and cook the *roux*, stirring, for 1 minute. Stir in the coconut milk gradually and cook the sauce over moderate heat, stirring constantly, until it is slightly thickened. Add the sauce to the shrimp and simmer the mixture for 2 minutes. Serve the shrimp over rice.

Serves 4 to 6.

Stone Harbor Crab Cakes

3/4 C. mayonnaise
1/4 C. sour cream
2 T. whole-grain mustard
1 large egg
2 lb. lump crab meat, cartilage removed
Canola oil
2 lemons, quartered

In a bowl whisk together the mayonnaise, sour cream, mustard, and egg, combining the mixture well. Gently fold in the crab meat and shape the mixture into eight 1-inch-thick cakes. Arrange the cakes on a baking sheet, oiled with canola oil, and bake them in a preheated 400° F. oven for 15 minutes, or until they are lightly browned. Turn the cakes with a spatula and broil them under a preheated broiler for 2 to 3 minutes, or until they are golden brown. Let the cakes stand for 5 minutes and transfer them to a heated platter. Garnish the crab cakes with the lemon wedges.

Serves 4.

Side by Side

Side by Side

Spring Artichokes

¹/₂ C. chopped mushroom
1¹/₂ T. minced shallot
4 T. butter
2 T. flour
³/₄ C. chicken broth
²/₃ C. minced ham
1 hard-boiled egg, chopped
1 T. minced fresh parsley
¹/₄ tsp. pepper
¹/₄ tsp. tarragon
1 (14-oz.) can artichoke bottoms, drained
¹/₃ C. bread crumbs
Sprigs of watercress

In a saucepan cook the mushroom and shallot in 3 tablespoons butter over moderate heat until they are softened, stir in the flour, and cook the mixture over low heat, stirring, until it is light brown. Stir in the broth and cook the mixture until it is thickened. Remove the pan from the heat and stir in the ham, egg, parsley, pepper, and tarragon.

Arrange the artichoke bottoms on a baking sheet and spoon 1 heaping tablespoon of the mushroom mixture into each bottom. Over low heat cook the crumbs in the remaining tablespoon butter for 1 minute and sprinkle the crumbs over the artichokes. Broil the artichokes under a preheated broiler 4 inches from the heat for 3 minutes, or until they are lightly browned. Transfer the artichokes to a platter and garnish them with the watercress.

Serves 8.

Asparagus Parmesan

1¼ lb. asparagus, trimmed
2 T. butter, softened
1½ tsp. minced parsley
2 tsp. minced fresh dill
1½ tsp. minced fresh rosemary, or ½ tsp. dried
Freshly ground white pepper to taste
2½ oz. grated Parmesan cheese

In a large saucepan of boiling water cook the asparagus for 1½ to 2 minutes, or until it is barely tender, and drain it. In a small bowl combine the butter, parsley, dill, rosemary, and pepper and pour the mixture over the asparagus in the warm pan. Toss the asparagus with the herbed butter until it is well coated and the butter is melted and transfer it to a warm serving plate. Sprinkle the asparagus with the Parmesan cheese.

Serves 4.

Sesame Asparagus

1 lb. asparagus, trimmed and peeled, if desired
¼ C. finely chopped red onion
1½ tsp. sesame seed
1½ tsp. sesame oil
Salt and freshly ground white pepper to taste

Arrange the asparagus on a microwave-safe plate and top it with the onion and sesame seed. Drizzle the oil over the asparagus and season it with the salt and pepper. Microwave the asparagus on high, covered with plastic wrap, for about 2 minutes, or to taste.

Serves 4.

Bourbon Baked Beans

3 cans red kidney beans, totaling 50 to 60 oz.
3 onions, sliced
1/4 C. wheat germ
1 apple, peeled, cored, and sliced
1/3 C. molasses
4 to 6 T. bourbon
3 garlic cloves, minced
1 tsp. ground mustard
1/2 tsp. salt
1/4 tsp. pepper
1/8 tsp. thyme
1/8 tsp. marjoram
3 whole cloves
1 tsp. Tabasco
3 slices lean bacon, cut into thirds

In a large bowl combine all the ingredients, transfer the mixture to a greased casserole, and bake it in a preheated 350° F. oven for 1 1/2 hours.

Serves 12.

A five hundred-year-old oak tree is a landmark in our historic town of Basking Ridge. Today it is ninety-seven feet high with a spread of one hundred fifty-six feet. In 1928 there was a cavity in the trunk large enough to hold three men, and it took three tons of concrete to fill it.

Stir-Fried Beans with Water Chestnuts

A simple way to dress up beans.

1 lb. green beans, strings removed and
    beans cut into 2-inch lengths
1½ T. peanut oil
1 tsp. salt
1½ tsp. sugar
10 water chestnuts, sliced
⅓ C. chicken broth
1 tsp. cornstarch dissolved in 2 T. stock or
    broth

In a wok or large skillet heat the oil, swirling it, for 40 seconds. Add the beans and stir-fry them for 3 minutes. Add the salt, sugar, and water chestnuts, stir the mixture, and pour in the broth. Cook the mixture over moderate heat, covered, for 2 to 3 minutes, or until the beans are tender but still crisp. Re-combine the cornstarch mixture, add it to the pan, and cook the beans until they are coated with a light glaze. Transfer the mixture to a heated platter.

Serves 4.

Sweet and Sour Red Cabbage

¾ lb. bacon, cut into 1-inch pieces
1½ C. chopped onion
1 small head red cabbage, cored and
    shredded
3 tart apples, peeled, cored, and chopped
⅔ C. red-wine vinegar
⅔ C. dry red wine
¾ C. golden raisins
2½ T. brown sugar
1 tsp. caraway seed
Salt and freshly ground pepper to taste

In a Dutch oven cook the bacon over moderate heat for 12 minutes, pour off some of the grease, and in the remaining grease cook the onion for about 10 minutes, or until it is softened. Stir in the cabbage, apples, red-wine vinegar, red wine, raisins, brown sugar, and caraway seed. Season the mixture with the salt and pepper and cook it, covered, for 1 hour and 15 minutes. Stir the mixture occasionally during the cooking and add more red wine if it becomes too dry. Transfer the mixture to a serving bowl and serve it hot.

Serves 8.

Vidalia Onion Gratinée

3 large Vidalia onions, sliced
3 T. extra virgin olive oil
1/2 (10³/4-oz.) can cream of celery soup
1/2 loaf French bread, cut into thick slices
Butter
1/2 to 3/4 C. grated Gruyère cheese

In a skillet sauté the onions in the oil until they are golden. Transfer them to a greased baking dish and spoon the soup over them. Butter enough bread slices to cover the top of the casserole and arrange them over the onions. Sprinkle the cheese over the bread and bake the dish in a preheated 350° F. oven for about 25 minutes, or until the bread is toasted.

Serves 6.

Basking Ridge's beautiful old oak tree has a circumference of eighteen feet. But we like to remember the preschoolers measuring it one day: it took twenty-nine of their sneakers placed heel to toe, plus two from their teachers, to encircle it.

Stuffed Eggplant

An excellent vegetarian main course or a flavorful side dish.

1 medium eggplant
1½ tsp. salt
3 T. extra virgin olive oil
1 C. finely chopped onion
1 T. minced garlic
⅔ C. fine dry bread crumbs
¼ C. pine nuts
¼ C. grated Parmesan cheese
¼ C. chopped celery
¼ C. minced fresh parsley
2 T. lemon juice

Halve the eggplant lengthwise and with a small sharp knife remove and reserve the pulp ½ inch from the peel, leaving a ½-inch shell. Sprinkle the shells with 1 teaspoon salt and invert them on paper towels to drain.

Coarsely chop the reserved eggplant pulp. In a large skillet heat 2 tablespoons of the olive oil, reserving the remaining tablespoon. Cook the eggplant, onion, and garlic over moderate heat, stirring frequently, for about 5 minutes. Remove the pan from the heat and stir in the remaining ingredients, except the reserved olive oil.

Rinse and pat dry the eggplant shells and divide the vegetable mixture between them. Put the stuffed eggplant in a baking pan, drizzle it with the reserved oil, and pour water into the pan to a depth of ¼ inch. Cover the pan tightly with foil and bake the eggplant in a preheated 350° F. oven for 40 minutes. Remove the foil and bake the eggplant for 12 minutes more, or until the edges are tender and the bread crumbs are lightly browned.

Serves 2 as an entrée or 4 as a first course or side dish.

Purée of Parsnips and Carrots

2 lb. parsnips, peeled and cut into chunks
2 lb. carrots, peeled and cut into chunks
¹/3 C. half-and-half
4 T. plus 1 tsp. butter, sliced
Salt and pepper to taste
¹/4 tsp. freshly grated nutmeg, or to taste

In a saucepan cook the parsnips and carrots in boiling salted water for about 25 minutes, or until they are tender. Drain the parsnips and carrots and transfer them to a food processor. Purée the vegetables, in batches if necessary, until the mixture is smooth.

In the pan melt the 4 tablespoons butter in the half-and-half and add the mixture to the purée, combining it well. Stir in the salt, pepper, and nutmeg and transfer the purée into a greased baking dish. Dot the top with the 1 teaspoon butter and bake the vegetables in a preheated 350° F. oven for 20 minutes.

Serves 6 to 8.

The earliest record of the name Basking Ridge can be found in the ecclesiastical records of The Presbyterian Church of Basking Ridge in the year 1733. According to legend, early settlers saw wild animals come up from the swampland and bask in the sun on the side of the ridge.

Herb Mashed Potatoes

4 potatoes, peeled and quartered
1/2 C. milk
1 T. minced fresh rosemary
1 tsp. minced fresh thyme
1/2 C. chopped scallion
2 T. unsalted butter
Salt and pepper to taste

In a saucepan boil the potatoes in water to cover until they are tender and drain them well. In a small saucepan scald the milk with the rosemary, thyme, and scallion, pour the mixture over the potatoes, and mash them. Add the butter and salt and pepper.

Serves 4.

Roasted Potatoes with Garlic and Parmesan

4 large baking potatoes, unpeeled
1/4 C. extra virgin olive oil
4 large garlic cloves, minced
1/2 C. grated Parmesan cheese

Cook the potatoes in a saucepan of boiling water, or in the microwave, until they are fork tender but still firm. Slice the potatoes lengthwise and put them in a bowl. In a small bowl stir together the olive oil and garlic, pour the oil over the potatoes, and toss them. Arrange the potatoes on a greased foil-lined baking sheet and roast them in a preheated 400° F. oven for 20 minutes. Sprinkle the potatoes with the cheese and roast them for 5 minutes more, or until they are brown and crisp.

Serves 6.

Sweet Potato Casserole

3 lb. sweet potatoes
1/4 C. orange juice
1/4 C. packed brown sugar
1/4 C. butter, melted
4 tsp. grated orange rind
1/2 tsp. cinnamon
1/4 tsp. nutmeg
1/4 tsp. ginger
2 large eggs
Salt and pepper to taste
Pecan halves for garnish

Prick the potatoes with a fork and bake them in a 400° F. oven for 1 hour, or until they are very tender. Peel the potatoes, cut them into chunks, and purée them in a food processor. Add the remaining ingredients, except the pecans. Purée the mixture until it is smooth, transfer it to a buttered casserole, and arrange the pecan halves on top. (At this point the casserole can be kept, covered and chilled, overnight.) Bake the casserole at 350° F. for about 30 minutes, or until it is just set and heated through.

Serves 6.

The first duty . . . Is to see that people have food, fuel, and clothes. The second, that they have means for moral and intellectual education.

Fors Clavigera (1876)

Butternut Squash with Apples and Maple Syrup

1 large tart green apple, peeled, cored, and
    cut into thin wedges
1 C. coarsely chopped onion
1 large garlic clove, minced
1 T. extra virgin olive oil
Pinch of nutmeg
Salt and pepper to taste
1 large butternut squash, peeled, halved
    lengthwise, seeded, and cut crosswise
    into 1/2-inch-thick slices
1 large egg
2 T. maple syrup

Arrange the apple, onion, and garlic in a
13- by 9- by 2-inch baking dish and drizzle the oil
over them. Sprinkle the mixture with the nutmeg
and salt and pepper and arrange the squash on
top. Bake the dish, covered tightly with foil, in a
preheated 350° F. oven for 1 hour, or until the
squash is very tender.

Do not turn off the oven. Transfer the squash
mixture with the juices to a food processor and
purée it until it is smooth. Correct the seasoning
and mix in the egg. Return the mixture to the
baking dish, drizzle the syrup over it, and bake it
for 25 minutes, or until the juices at the edge just
begin to bubble.

Serves 6.

Artichoke-Stuffed Tomatoes

2 1/3 C. day-old coarse bread crumbs
2/3 C. chopped onion
5 T. butter
1 C. finely chopped artichoke bottoms
Salt and pepper to taste
4 large tomatoes, halved, seeded, and cored

In a skillet sauté the bread crumbs and onion
in the butter until the crumbs begin to turn golden.
Add the artichoke bottoms and salt and pepper and
cook the mixture until it is hot. Stuff the tomatoes
with the mixture and bake them in a preheated
350° F. oven for 30 minutes.

Serves 6 to 8.

Broiled Sherry Tomatoes

Quick, easy, attractive, and a little different.

4 large tomatoes, halved, seeded, and cored
1/3 C. dry Sherry
4 tsp. minced fresh dill, or 2 tsp. dried
Salt and freshly grated pepper to taste
8 tsp. mayonnaise
1 C. grated sharp Cheddar cheese

Pierce the flesh of each tomato several times with a fork and sprinkle each half with about 2 teaspoons Sherry, 1/2 teaspoon fresh dill, or 1/4 teaspoon dried, and the salt and pepper. Broil the tomatoes under a preheated broiler for 2 to 3 minutes. Top each tomato half with 1 teaspoon mayonnaise and 2 tablespoons cheese and broil them for 2 to 3 minutes more, or until the cheese is bubbly.

Serves 6 to 8.

Better is a dish of vegetables where love is, than a fatted ox and hatred with it.

Proverbs 15:17

Herbed Zucchini and Carrots

1/4 C. extra virgin olive oil
3 shallots, minced
6 large carrots, cut into julienne strips
2 T. water
1/2 tsp. sugar
2 large zucchini, cut into julienne strips
2 T. minced fresh mint
2 T. minced fresh parsley
2 T. minced fresh sage
Salt and freshly ground pepper to taste

In a large skillet heat the oil over moderate heat and in it cook the shallots until they are soft. Add the carrots, 2 tablespoons water, and sugar and cook the mixture over moderately low heat, covered, shaking the pan frequently, for about 10 minutes, or until the carrots begin to soften. Add the zucchini and cook the mixture, uncovered, stirring frequently, for 3 to 4 minutes more, or until the zucchini is slightly softened. Stir in the mint, parsley, sage, and salt and pepper and serve the vegetables hot or at room temperature.

Serves 8.

Sautéed Zucchini and Yellow Squash

1 onion, chopped
2 1/2 T. extra virgin olive oil
2 yellow squash, sliced
2 zucchini, sliced
1 red pepper, seeded and chopped
1 tsp. oregano
1/2 tsp. basil
Salt and freshly ground pepper to taste
1/2 C. crumbled chèvre
1/3 C. pitted Greek olives
2 tsp. lemon juice

In a large skillet sauté the onion in the olive oil for 5 minutes. Add the squash, zucchini, and pepper and stir-fry the mixture over moderately high heat for 5 to 6 minutes, or until the vegetables are barely tender. Add the oregano, basil, and salt and pepper and stir in the cheese and olives. Sprinkle the mixture with the lemon juice, transfer it to a serving plate, and serve it warm or at room temperature.

Serves 6 to 8.

Vegetable Potpourri

3 carrots, chopped
1 yellow squash, halved lengthwise and sliced
2 lb. broccoli, stems reserved for another use and
    top cut into small florets
1 red pepper, seeded and finely chopped
1 C. frozen peas, thawed
Grated rind of 1 lemon
1½ T. minced parsley
⅔ C. Vinaigrette Dressing (page 40)

In a saucepan of boiling water cook the carrots for 1 minute. Remove them with a slotted spoon, rinse them under cold water, and reserve them. Cook the squash in the same water for 30 seconds. Remove the squash with a slotted spoon, rinse it under cold water, and reserve it. Cook the broccoli in the same water for 30 seconds. Remove the broccoli with a slotted spoon, rinse it under cold water, and reserve it. Pat all the vegetables dry with paper towels.

In a large bowl combine the carrots, squash and broccoli with the pepper, peas, lemon rind, and parsley, and toss everything with the Vinaigrette Dressing.

Serves 6.

Do not neglect to show hospitality to strangers, for by doing that some have entertained angels without knowing it.

Hebrews 13:2

Sausage-Stuffed Zucchini

The bounty of your summer garden makes this a colorful dish.

3 (1-lb.) zucchini, ends trimmed
1¼ teaspoons salt
1 red pepper
1 lb. sweet Italian sausage, casings removed
1 large onion, chopped
1 ear of corn, kernels removed
4 slices of bread, coarsely crumbled
2 large eggs, lightly beaten
½ C. grated sharp cheese
2 T. minced fresh parsley
⅛ tsp. pepper
Shredded Fontina cheese to taste

In a large pot cook the whole zucchini in boiling water to cover with ½ teaspoon salt until it is just tender, but do not overcook it. Halve the zucchini lengthwise and with a melon-ball cutter or spoon carefully remove and reserve the centers. Invert the scooped-out shells and let them drain on paper towels.

On a greased baking sheet broil the red pepper, turning it as it chars, until it is lightly charred on all sides. (Watch carefully, for it will burn easily.) Let the pepper cool enough to handle and peel, seed, and chop it.

In a skillet sauté the sausage, separating it into small bits, until it is browned. Transfer it with a slotted spoon to paper towels to drain. Add the onion to the skillet, sauté it until it is golden, and transfer it with the slotted spoon to a bowl. Add the scooped-out part of the zucchini, mashing it into small bits, and stir in the sausage, corn, red pepper, bread, eggs, cheese, parsley, pepper, and remaining salt, combining the mixture well.

Put the zucchini shells in an oiled shallow baking dish, divide the stuffing among them, and sprinkle the tops with the Fontina cheese. Bake the zucchini in a preheated 350° F. oven for 45 minutes.

Serves 6.

Summer Vegetable Medley

2 T. extra virgin olive oil
2 zucchini, trimmed and sliced into thin rounds
2 yellow squash, trimmed and sliced into thin
     rounds
1 onion, finely chopped
2 garlic cloves, minced
$\frac{1}{2}$ tsp. thyme
3 tomatoes, cored and thinly sliced
Salt and freshly ground pepper to taste
2 T. minced fresh basil
3 T. grated Parmesan cheese

Heat 1 tablespoon olive oil in a nonstick skillet and
in it sauté the zucchini, yellow squash, onion, garlic, and
thyme, tossing the vegetables gently, for 5 minutes.
Transfer the mixture to a greased casserole, arrange the
tomatoes decoratively on top, and sprinkle them with the
salt and pepper, basil, and cheese. Drizzle the remaining
oil over the top. Bake the dish in a preheated 450° F. oven
for 5 to 8 minutes, or until the top is bubbly and
beginning to brown.

Serves 4.

*To entertain a guest is to
make yourself responsible
for his happiness so long as
he is beneath your roof.*

Brillat-Savarin

Vegetable Paella

A terrific accompaniment to chicken or pork.

2 onions, finely chopped
2 garlic cloves, minced
1 T. extra virgin olive oil
1 tsp. oregano
$1/2$ tsp. ground cumin
Dash of Tabasco
$1^1/2$ C. uncooked long-grain rice
3 C. chicken broth
1 red pepper, seeded and chopped
1 yellow pepper, seeded and chopped
4 C. chopped spinach, or 1 (10-oz.) package
   frozen spinach, thawed, and squeezed
   dry
1 ($15^1/2$-oz.) can cannellini, drained and
   rinsed
$1/4$ C. finely chopped sun-dried tomatoes
Salt and pepper to taste

In a large saucepan cook the onions and garlic in the oil over moderate heat for 6 minutes, or until they are softened. Stir in the oregano, cumin, Tabasco, and rice, pour in the broth, and bring the liquid to a boil. Reduce the heat to low and simmer the mixture, covered, for 10 minutes. Add the peppers and spinach and simmer the mixture for 5 minutes. Add the cannellini, tomatoes, and salt and pepper and simmer the mixture for 5 to 10 minutes, or until the rice is tender.

Serves 6.

Pastas and Grains

Pastas and Grains

Fettuccine with Scallops

1 lb. asparagus, trimmed and cut into
    1¹/2-inch pieces
¹/2 lb. small green beans (preferably *haricots
    verts*), trimmed and cut into 1¹/2-inch
    pieces
1 lb. fettuccine
3 T. butter
1 (10-oz.) package frozen peas, thawed
2 lb. sea scallops, quartered
1¹/2 C. Basil Pesto, or prepared pesto sauce
³/4 C. heavy cream
2 T. lemon juice
Salt and pepper to taste

In a large pot of boiling salted water cook the asparagus and beans for about 5 minutes, or until they are crisp-tender. Transfer the vegetables with a strainer to a large bowl and in the pot cook the fettuccine, stirring occasionally, until it is *al dente*.

In a large skillet melt half the butter over moderately high heat, add the asparagus, beans, peas, and salt and pepper to taste, and heat the mixture, stirring, until it is hot. Transfer the vegetables to the bowl. In the skillet melt the remaining butter, add the scallops and salt and pepper to taste, and sauté them for 1 minute. Drain the pasta and add it to the skillet with the vegetables, pesto, cream, and lemon juice. Heat the mixture over low heat, stirring, season it with salt and pepper, and transfer it to serving plates.

Serves 8.

Basil Pesto

Use pesto as a delicious pasta sauce, on pizza, as a sandwich spread, or as a delicious enhancement to any tomato-based sauce.

4 C. medium-packed basil leaves
²/3 C. chopped walnuts
²/3 C. grated Parmesan cheese
1 garlic clove
¹/2 tsp. salt
¹/2 C. extra virgin olive oil, or to taste
Freshly ground pepper to taste

In a food processor mince the basil leaves. Add the walnuts, cheese, garlic, and salt and purée the mixture. Pour the oil slowly through the feed tube and process the mixture until the oil is well incorporated. Add the pepper, correct the seasoning, and add more oil, 1 teaspoon at a time, until the pesto has the desired consistency.

Makes about 1¹/2 cups.

Vegetable Lasagna with Mushroom Sauce

1 oz. dried wild mushrooms
1 C. finely chopped onion
1 T. extra virgin olive oil
4 oz. fresh mushrooms, sliced
1/2 C. minced Italian parsley
2 tsp. minced fresh rosemary, or 1 tsp. dried
1 (28-oz.) can crushed plum tomatoes
Salt and freshly ground pepper to taste
10 pre-cooked lasagna noodles
8 oz. shredded part-skim mozzarella cheese
1/4 C. grated Parmesan cheese

In a small bowl combine the dried mushrooms with 1 cup boiling water and let them stand for 30 minutes. Remove the mushrooms, reserving the water, trim the stems, and slice the tops. In a large skillet cook the onion in the oil over moderate heat for about 5 minutes, or until it is soft, add the fresh mushrooms, and cook the mixture until the liquid is absorbed. Stir in the parsley, rosemary, tomatoes, dried mushrooms, and reserved liquid and season the mixture with the salt and pepper. Simmer the sauce for 20 minutes.

Spread several tablespoons of the sauce in the bottom of an oiled 9- by 13-inch baking dish and cover it with a layer of noodles, half the Cheese Filling, half the mozzarella, and half the Vegetable Filling. Spoon 1 cup of the sauce over the vegetables and repeat the layering. Add remaining noodles and spread them with remaining sauce. Sprinkle the top with the Parmesan cheese and bake the lasagna, covered with foil, in a preheated 350° F. oven for 30 minutes. Remove the foil and bake for 15 minutes more. Let the lasagna stand for 10 minutes before serving. The lasagna can be prepared ahead and frozen or made in the morning and baked just before serving.

Serves 8.

Cheese Filling

1 (15-oz.) carton part-skim ricotta cheese
1 (10-oz.) package chopped spinach, drained and squeezed dry
1/2 C. low-fat buttermilk
1 C. grated Parmesan cheese
Salt and freshly ground pepper to taste

In a bowl combine all the ingredients until the filling is well blended and reserve the mixture.

Vegetable Filling

2 red peppers and 1 green pepper, roasted, peeled, seeded, and julienned
1 yellow squash, thinly sliced and lightly steamed
2 zucchini, thinly sliced and lightly steamed
1 eggplant, thinly sliced, sprayed or wiped with canola oil, and broiled until lightly browned
1 (13-oz.) can artichoke hearts
1/2 lemon
1/2 C. chicken broth
1/2 C. thinly sliced onion

In a large bowl combine the peppers, squash, zucchini, and eggplant and squeeze lemon juice over the artichokes to keep them from discoloring. In a skillet cook the artichokes in the chicken broth over moderately high heat for about 2 minutes. Transfer the artichokes with a slotted spoon to the vegetable mixture. Cook the onion in the remaining chicken broth until it is softened and add it to the vegetable mixture.

Salmon Linguine

4 T. butter
1/2 C. flour
2 envelopes or cubes chicken bouillon
1 C. water
2 C. milk
1/4 C. dry white wine
2 tsp. *fines herbes*
Salt and freshly ground pepper to taste
1 1/2 lb. salmon fillets, cut into bite-size pieces
2 bunches scallions, chopped
2 T. extra virgin olive oil
1/3 C. dry white wine
8 oz. fresh sugar snap peas
8 oz. tiny French beans
1 lb. fresh linguine
Minced fresh parsley to taste

In a saucepan melt the butter, stir in the flour, and cook the *roux* over moderate heat, stirring, for 3 minutes. Dissolve the bouillon in the water and slowly stir it into the *roux* with the milk and wine. Simmer the sauce, stirring occasionally, for 5 minutes. Add the *fines herbes* and salt and pepper and keep the sauce warm.

In a skillet sauté the salmon and scallions in the olive oil for 2 minutes, add the wine, and cook the mixture until the salmon is just done, being careful not to overcook it.

In a steamer steam the peas and beans until they are just crisp and remove them from the heat.

In a large pot of boiling salted water cook the linguine for 2 minutes, or until it is *al dente*. Drain it and return it to the pot. Add the salmon mixture, the vegetables, and the sauce and toss the mixture. Transfer the pasta to a platter and sprinkle it with the minced parsley.

Serves 4 to 6.

The Paige Whitney Babies Center has been in existence since 1992 and has given assistance to almost two thousand families. Every phase of the operation is accomplished by volunteers.

Thai Shrimp Pasta

Just one tablespoon of pepper flakes makes this an exceedingly spicy dish — but for those who like things truly searing, pour on even more. The sauce can take it.

- 1 lb. peeled deveined shrimp, cooked and still warm
- 1/4 C. lime juice
- 1/2 C. peanut butter
- 1/2 C. soy sauce
- 1/2 C. chicken broth
- 2 T. honey
- 1 T. crushed dried red pepper flakes, or to taste
- 1/2 tsp. salt
- 1 lb. linguine, cooked according to package directions
- 1/2 C. chopped scallion

In a large bowl combine the lime juice, peanut butter, soy sauce, broth, honey, pepper, and salt and add the shrimp. Toss the mixture with the pasta, transfer it to a platter, and sprinkle it with the scallion.

Serves 4 to 6.

Orzo with Gruyère and Dill

- 1 T. lemon zest
- 1/2 C. minced shallot
- 1/2 C. finely chopped celery
- 1 T. butter
- 2 T. extra virgin olive oil
- 3 T. flour
- 2 C. chicken broth
- Salt and pepper to taste
- 1 lb. orzo
- 1/3 C. minced fresh dill
- 2 C. grated Gruyère cheese (about 6 oz.)

Sprinkle a buttered 2-quart shallow baking dish with 2 teaspoons lemon zest. In a saucepan sauté the shallot and celery in the butter and oil until the celery is softened. Add the flour and cook the mixture, stirring, for 3 minutes. Add the broth and bring the mixture to a boil, stirring. Add the remaining zest and salt and pepper to taste and cook the mixture, stirring, for 3 minutes.

In a pot of boiling salted water cook the orzo for about 6 minutes, or until it is just *al dente*, and drain it. Return the orzo to the pot and stir in the broth mixture. Stir in the dill and cheese and transfer the mixture to the baking dish. Bake the orzo in a preheated 350° F. oven for 30 minutes, or until it is bubbly and the top is slightly crusty.

Serves 6 to 8 as a side dish.

Penne with Artichokes, Peppers, and Asparagus

2 red peppers
1 lb. penne
1 lb. asparagus, trimmed and cut into 2-inch
    pieces
1 (13-oz.) can quartered artichoke hearts
2 tsp. extra virgin olive oil
3 T. butter
1/4 C. flour
3 C. milk
1½ C. grated Fontina cheese
2 C. grated Parmesan cheese
Salt and freshly ground pepper to taste
1 oz. arugula, chopped

In a broiler char the peppers until they are blackened on all sides. Let them stand for 10 minutes, peel and seed them, and cut them into 1/2-inch pieces.

Cook the penne in a large pot of boiling salted water, stirring occasionally, for 10 minutes, add the asparagus and artichokes, and cook the pasta for 4 minutes more, or until it is just *al dente*.

Drain the pasta and vegetables, transfer them to a large bowl, and toss them with the olive oil.

In a saucepan melt the butter, stir in the flour, and cook the *roux* over moderate heat, stirring, for 2 minutes. Gradually whisk in the milk and continue to whisk the sauce until it is smooth. Cook the sauce, whisking frequently, for about 8 minutes, remove the pan from the heat, and whisk in the Fontina and 1½ cups Parmesan. Season the sauce with the salt and pepper.

Add the sauce and the arugula to the pasta and toss the mixture well. Transfer the pasta to a platter and sprinkle it with the remaining Parmesan cheese.

Serves 6.

A rewarding development of The Paige Whitney Babies Center is that thirty-five women have taken advantage of academic scholarships offered by the Center, totaling over $53,000.

Goat Cheese and Shiitake Mushroom Ravioli with Roasted Tomato Sauce

4 oz. shiitake mushrooms, minced
3 T. butter
6 oz. goat cheese
2 T. minced fresh basil
1 large garlic clove, minced
32 won ton wrappers
1 large egg, lightly beaten with 1 tsp. water
1/3 C. freshly grated Parmesan cheese

In a skillet sauté the mushrooms in the butter over moderate heat until they are just softened and in a bowl combine them with the goat cheese. Add the basil and garlic and combine the mixture well.

Put 4 won ton wrappers on a cutting board, keeping the remaining wrappers covered with plastic wrap, and put a rounded teaspoon of the cheese mixture in the middle of two of the wrappers. Brush the exposed surfaces with the egg wash and top the filling with the unfilled wrappers, pressing the edges tightly to seal them. With a 3-inch-round cookie cutter or a sharp knife cut rounds from the squares, pinching the edges to seal them when necessary. Lay the ravioli in one layer between sheets of plastic wrap as they are made and chill them until they are ready to be cooked. Fill and cut the remaining wrappers in the same manner.

In a large pot of boiling water cook the ravioli for 3 to 4 minutes, or until they are just tender. Drain the ravioli on paper towels, divide them among four serving plates, and top each serving with a small amount of Roasted Tomato Sauce. Put the Parmesan in a small serving dish and pass it at the table.

Serves 4.

Roasted Tomato Sauce

1 1/2 lb. ripe tomatoes (about 4 large)
4 large garlic cloves, unpeeled
1 onion, halved
Salt and freshly ground pepper to taste
2 T. freshly grated Parmesan cheese

Put the tomatoes, garlic, and onion on an oiled jelly-roll pan and roast them at 400° F. for 20 minutes, or until the tomatoes are soft and the skins are just beginning to split. Let the vegetables cool slightly.

Remove the skins from the garlic, squeezing the pulp into a blender or food processor, and add the onions. Peel the tomatoes, discarding the skins, and add them to the blender or food processor. Purée the vegetables until they are smooth.

Transfer the purée to a small saucepan and simmer it over moderate heat, stirring frequently, for 20 minutes, or until it is thick. Add the salt and pepper and Parmesan cheese.

Rigatoni with Green Olives and Feta Cheese

5 T. extra virgin olive oil
1½ C. onion, chopped
2 garlic cloves, minced
3 (28-oz.) cans crushed tomatoes
1 T. minced fresh basil
1 tsp. crushed dried red pepper
2 C. low-sodium chicken broth
Salt and pepper to taste
1 lb. rigatoni
2¼ C. crumbled Feta cheese
⅔ C. chopped green Spanish olives
⅓ C. grated Parmesan cheese

In a large saucepan or Dutch oven heat 3 tablespoons olive oil and in it sauté the onion and garlic over moderately high heat for about 5 minutes. Stir in the tomatoes, basil, pepper, and broth and bring the mixture to a boil. Reduce the heat and simmer the sauce, stirring occasionally, for about 1½ hours, or until it is reduced and thickened. Add salt and pepper to taste.

In a large pot cook the rigatoni according to the package directions until it is just *al dente*. Drain the pasta and return it to the pot. Toss it with the remaining oil, pour the sauce over it, and mix in the Feta and olives. Transfer the pasta to a platter and sprinkle it with the Parmesan.

Serves 6.

Tie sprigs of rosemary with pretty bows and set one at each place as a sign of friendship and remembrance.

Smoked Turkey and Toasted Walnut Ravioli with Gorgonzola Cream Sauce

6 oz. smoked turkey or chicken, minced
1/4 C. chopped walnuts, toasted
1/2 C. ricotta cheese
2 T. freshly grated Parmesan cheese
1/4 tsp. thyme
Salt and freshly ground pepper to taste
1 large egg
48 won ton wrappers
1 large egg beaten with 1 tsp. water

In a bowl combine the turkey, walnuts, cheeses, thyme, salt, pepper, and egg and blend the mixture well.

Prepare won ton wrappers, fill them with the turkey mixture, and cook the ravioli as for *Goat Cheese and Shiitake Mushroom Ravioli* (page 114). Divide the ravioli among six plates and top each serving with Gorgonzola Cream Sauce.

Serves 6.

Gorgonzola Cream Sauce

2 shallots, minced
2 T. butter
1/3 C. dry white wine
1 1/4 C. heavy cream
3 oz. Gorgonzola, crumbled

In a small saucepan sauté the shallots in the butter until they are softened, add the wine, and bring the mixture to a boil. Reduce it by half, add the cream, and boil the mixture until it is slightly thickened and reduced to about 1 1/4 cups. Remove the pan from the heat, stir in the cheese, and stir the sauce until the cheese is melted, returning the pan to the heat briefly if necessary. Spoon the sauce over the ravioli or transfer it to a serving dish.

Dried Tomato, Mushroom, and Artichoke Heart Pasta

3 T. butter
1 (16-oz.) can diced tomatoes
3/4 C. half-and-half
1/2 C. vodka
1/4 tsp. dried crushed red pepper
Salt and freshly ground black pepper to taste
2 T. extra virgin olive oil
1/2 lb. mushrooms, trimmed and sliced
3/4 C. chopped drained sun-dried tomatoes
    packed in oil
1 (13-oz.) can quartered artichoke hearts, drained
1 1/2 T. minced shallot
2 tsp. minced fresh basil
1 lb. rigatoni
Grated Parmesan cheese

In a skillet melt the butter, stir in the tomatoes, half-and-half, vodka, and red pepper, and let the mixture simmer for about 8 minutes, or until it is slightly thickened. Add the salt and pepper and keep the sauce warm.

In another skillet sauté the mushrooms in the oil for about 4 minutes, add the dried tomatoes, artichokes, shallot, and basil, and cook the mixture, stirring, for 2 minutes. Stir in the sauce, cook the mixture over moderate heat, stirring occasionally, for 5 minutes, and correct the seasoning.

In a large pot cook the pasta according to the package directions until it is just *al dente* and drain it, reserving 1/2 cup of the cooking liquid. Return the pasta to the pot, pour the sauce and reserved cooking liquid over it, and toss the pasta. Transfer the pasta to a platter and sprinkle it with the cheese.

Serves 4 to 6.

Tiny and neat, handmade lavender bags can be stitched from fabric and lace scraps, or made up to match a scented hanger. Different shapes can be filled with dried lavender, lemon verbena, mint or rose petals, or a fragrant mixture.

Spinach Rotelle with Ham and Mushrooms

6 oz. mushrooms, trimmed and sliced
6 T. butter
12 oz. spinach rotelle
1/4 C. flour
1 1/4 C. milk
1 1/4 C. low-sodium chicken broth
1/4 tsp. freshly grated nutmeg
Salt and freshly ground white pepper to taste
4 oz. Gruyère cheese, shredded
4 oz. lean ham, finely chopped

In a skillet sauté the mushrooms in 2 tablespoons butter, stirring occasionally, for about 5 minutes, and reserve them.

In a saucepan melt 2 1/2 tablespoons butter over moderate heat. Add the flour and cook the *roux*, stirring, for 2 minutes. Gradually stir in the milk and broth, bring the sauce to a bare simmer, and continue to cook and stir the mixture over moderate heat for 8 to 10 minutes, or until it is slightly thickened and creamy. Add the mushrooms, nutmeg, and salt and pepper.

In a large pot cook the rotelle in boiling salted water until it is just *al dente*, drain it, and return it to the pot. Toss it with 1 1/2 tablespoons butter.

Spread one third of the pasta in a buttered 8- by 12-inch ovenproof dish and top it with one third of the ham and cheese. Spoon on one third of the sauce and repeat the layering once. Spread the remaining pasta with the remaining ham, and sauce and sprinkle the dish with remaining cheese. Bake the dish in a preheated 350° F. oven for 20 to 25 minutes, or until it is heated through.

Serves 6.

Spaghetti with Anchovies and Tuna

3/4 lb. spaghetti
3 T. extra virgin olive oil
4 canned fillets of anchovies with capers
1 1/2 T. minced garlic
2 (14-oz.) cans chopped tomatoes
1/2 C. dry white wine
1 (13-oz.) can white tuna packed in water, drained
1/4 C. minced fresh parsley
Salt and pepper to taste

In a large pot of boiling salted water cook the pasta according to the package directions until it is just *al dente*, drain it, and return it to the pot.

While the pasta is cooking heat the oil in a skillet over moderate heat and in it cook the anchovies and garlic, mashing them to a paste, for 2 minutes. Add the tomatoes and wine and cook the mixture over moderately high heat for about 5 minutes, or until the sauce thickens slightly. Add the tuna and parsley, breaking up the chunks of tuna with a fork, and combine the sauce well. Season the sauce with the salt and pepper.

Pour the sauce over the pasta, toss the pasta with the sauce, and transfer the pasta to a platter.

Serves 4.

Couscous with Toasted Almonds and Dried Apricots

1¹/₂ C. water
2 T. extra virgin olive oil
1 tsp. salt
1 C. plus 2 T. couscous
²/₃ C. chopped dried apricots
1¹/₂ tsp. cinnamon
¹/₄ tsp. allspice
¹/₂ C. chopped scallion
²/₃ C. sliced almonds, lightly toasted

In a saucepan combine the water, oil, and salt and bring the liquid to a boil. In a bowl combine the couscous, apricots, and spices and pour the boiling liquid over them. Cover the bowl and let the mixture stand for about 5 minutes, or until the liquid is absorbed. Fluff the couscous with a fork. (The couscous should have increased in size and become very fluffy. If it is not very fluffy, add ¹/₄ cup more boiling water and let the mixture stand, covered, for 5 minutes more.) Stir in the scallion and almonds and serve the dish warm or at room temperature.

Serves 4 to 6.

For a festive air, tie thin ribbon bows and a few sprigs of pepper berries or thyme around the stems of wineglasses.

Risotto with Fresh Mushrooms

12 mushrooms
6 to 8 cups beef broth or mixed meat stock
1 stick butter
1 onion, finely chopped
2 C. Arborio (short-grained Italian rice) or
    brown rice
3/4 C. Pinot Grigio wine
3/4 C. grated Parmesan cheese
2 T. minced fresh parsley

Separate the mushroom stems from the caps,
slice the caps, and in a saucepan simmer the broth
with the stems for at least 30 minutes. Let the broth
continue to simmer while the rice cooks.

In another saucepan melt 6 tablespoons butter
over low heat, add the onion, and cook it, stirring,
until it is translucent. Add the rice, increase the heat
slightly, and stir the mixture to coat the rice with the
butter. Stir in the wine and let it sizzle until it
evaporates. Ladle 1 cup of the simmering broth
over the rice and let the rice absorb it, stirring
frequently. Repeat the process, adding broth 1 cup
at a time, for 10 to 12 minutes, or until the rice is
about half cooked.

Fold the mushroom caps into the rice and
continue to ladle in broth, letting the rice absorb it,
for another 8 to 10 minutes, or until the rice is
al dente. (Add only as much broth as the rice can
absorb without overcooking.) Remove the pan
from the heat and stir in the cheese, parsley, and
remaining butter. Let the risotto stand, covered, for
1 to 2 minutes and serve it with extra Parmesan
cheese.

Serves 4.

Risotto with Sausage

6 to 8 C. vegetable stock or broth
4 T. butter
Freshly ground pepper to taste
1 white onion, chopped
2 C. Arborio (short-grained Italian rice) or
    brown rice
1 lb. sweet Italian sausage, casings removed
1 C. Chianti
6 fresh sage leaves, minced
Leaves from 3 (2-inch) sprigs of rosemary,
    minced
3/4 C. grated Parmesan cheese

In a large saucepan heat the stock or broth and
keep it at a simmer.

In a saucepan melt 3 tablespoons butter, add
the pepper and onion, and cook the onion until it is
translucent. Stir in the rice and sausage and sauté
the mixture until the sausage is cooked. Add the
Chianti and cook the mixture until the wine
evaporates. Add 1 cup of the simmering broth and
cook the mixture, stirring frequently, until the broth
is absorbed. Continue adding broth, 1 cup at a time,
until the rice is *al dente.* (Add only as much broth as
the rice can absorb without overcooking.) Stir in the
sage and rosemary, remove the pan from the heat,
and stir in the remaining butter and the Parmesan.
Let the mixture stand, covered, for 1 to 2 minutes
before serving. Serve the risotto with extra
Parmesan cheese.

Serves 4.

Risotto with Artichoke Hearts and Hazelnuts

Asparagus and pine nuts can be substituted for the peas and hazelnuts. With a green salad, a country loaf, and a fruit dessert, this comforting dish makes a memorable winter meal.

1 small onion, chopped
2 T. extra virgin olive oil
1 garlic clove, minced
3 C. chicken broth
1 C. water
3/4 C. Arborio rice (short-grained Italian rice)
2 (13-oz.) cans quartered artichoke hearts, drained
Juice of 1/2 lemon
1 C. peas
1/2 C. chopped skinned hazelnuts, toasted
1/2 C. grated Parmesan cheese
Salt and freshly ground pepper to taste

In a large saucepan sauté the onion in 1 tablespoon olive oil until it is translucent. Add the garlic and cook the mixture for 1 minute.

In another saucepan bring the chicken broth and water to a simmer. To the larger pan add the rice and the remaining olive oil and cook the mixture, stirring, for 2 minutes. Add about 1/2 cup of the broth and water and cook the mixture, stirring, until the liquid is absorbed. Add about 1/2 cup more broth and repeat the process, stirring and cooking after each addition until the liquid is absorbed. Cook the rice for about 20 minutes, or until it is *al dente.* (Add only as much broth as the rice can absorb without overcooking.) With the last addition of liquid, stir in the artichokes, lemon juice, peas, nuts, cheese, and salt and pepper. The rice should be served very moist but still holding its shape and not runny. Transfer the risotto to a serving plate and serve it immediately.

Serves 4.

Artichokes, fresh or dried, are always an attractive addition to a centerpiece. Try an antique urn filled with artichokes, some wild bittersweet, and a few sprigs of greens.

Polenta Pie with Three Cheeses

3 C. water
1 C. yellow cornmeal
$1/2$ tsp. salt
2 T. Parmesan cheese

In a large saucepan combine the water, cornmeal, and salt, bring the water to a boil over high heat, stirring constantly, and cook the mixture until it is thickened. Reduce the heat to moderately low and cook the mixture for 10 minutes. Remove the pan from the heat, stir in the Parmesan, and pour the mixture into a greased 9-inch pie plate. With dampened hands pat the mixture evenly over the bottom and sides of the plate and bake it in a preheated 425° F. oven for 25 minutes.

Filling

2 large eggs
1 lb. ricotta cheese
$3/4$ C. grated mozzarella cheese
2 T. flour
1 T. minced fresh parsley
$1/2$ tsp. basil
$1/2$ tsp. salt
Freshly ground pepper to taste
1 T. Parmesan cheese

In a bowl beat the eggs lightly and beat in the ricotta, mozzarella, flour, parsley, basil, salt, and pepper. Pour the mixture into the shell and sprinkle it with the Parmesan. Bake the pie at 350° F. for 20 to 25 minutes, or until the filling is set, and put it under the broiler for 2 to 3 minutes, or until the top is golden. Serve the pie with Chunky Tomato Sauce.

Serves 6.

Chunky Tomato Sauce

2 carrots, chopped
2 small zucchini, chopped
1 onion, chopped
2 garlic cloves, minced
$1/2$ tsp. basil
$1/2$ tsp. oregano
Dash Tabasco
Salt and pepper to taste
1 T. extra virgin olive oil
1 (28-oz.) can tomatoes
3 T. tomato paste

In a large skillet cook the carrots, zucchini, onion, garlic, basil, oregano, Tabasco, salt, and pepper in the oil over moderate heat for 5 minutes. Stir in the tomatoes with the juice and the tomato paste, mashing and breaking apart the tomatoes, and cook the sauce over high heat for 10 minutes, or until it is thickened.

Makes about 3 cups.

Chili Rice Casserole

Rich, but oh so good. If you live in the South, where hominy is available, try substituting it for the rice.

2¹/₂ C. long-grain rice, cooked
1¹/₄ C. sour cream (nonfat can be substituted)
1¹/₄ C. plain yogurt (low-fat can be substituted)
2 (4¹/₂-oz.) cans chopped mild green chilies
Salt and freshly ground pepper to taste
³/₄ lb. extra-sharp Cheddar cheese, grated

In a bowl combine the warm rice with the sour cream, yogurt, and chilies. Add the salt and pepper and in a large greased casserole layer the mixture with the cheese, reserving ¹/₂ cup cheese. Bake the casserole at 350° F. for 25 minutes. Sprinkle the top with the reserved cheese and bake the casserole for 5 minutes more.

Serves 8.

Healing is a matter of time, but it is sometimes also a matter of opportunity.

Hippocrates (c. 460–400 B.C.),
Precepts

Polenta with Peppers and Bacon

Equally well received as main or side dish.

1 C. white cornmeal
3 C. water
1/2 tsp. salt
1/3 C. grated Parmesan cheese
1/4 C. extra virgin olive oil
2 onions, chopped
1 large red pepper, seeded and chopped
1 large orange pepper, seeded and chopped
1 large yellow pepper, seeded and chopped
1/2 C. dry white wine
1 (15-oz.) can tomato sauce
1/2 lb. bacon, fried crisp and crumbled
Salt and freshly ground pepper to taste
3 to 4 tablespoons extra virgin olive oil
3 oz. goat cheese, crumbled

In a small bowl stir the cornmeal into 1 cup water. In a saucepan bring the remaining 2 cups water to a boil with the salt and stir in the cornmeal mixture. Cook the mixture over moderate heat, stirring, for about 3 minutes, turn off the heat, and stir in the Parmesan cheese. Scrape the mixture into a well-greased 8-inch-square pan, let it cool for about 15 minutes, and chill it until it is well set. (This step may be done up to 8 hours before serving.)

In a skillet sauté the onions in 2 tablespoons oil until they are softened, add the remaining 2 tablespoons oil and the peppers, and cook the mixture, stirring occasionally, for about 3 minutes. Add the wine and tomato sauce, reduce the heat to low, and cook the mixture, covered, for about 20 minutes. Stir in the bacon and season the sauce with the salt and pepper.

Invert the pan of polenta onto a cutting board, tapping it against the board, if necessary, to dislodge it, and cut it into rectangles. In another skillet sauté the rectangles in 2 tablespoons oil, turning them once and adding more oil, if necessary, until they are golden on both sides, and transfer them to a platter. Spoon the sauce over the polenta and sprinkle the top with the goat cheese.

Serves 6.

Breads and Breakfast

Breads and Breakfast

Banana Bread

A classic, but this one's low in fat.

  1 C. sugar
  2 large eggs
  $^1/_4$ C. vegetable oil
  $^1/_4$ C. applesauce
  2 C. flour
  1$^1/_2$ tsp. baking powder
  $^1/_2$ tsp. salt
  $^1/_2$ tsp. baking soda
  $^1/_2$ C. water
  1 C. mashed bananas (about 2)
  $^1/_2$ C. chopped walnuts

In a large bowl beat the sugar with the eggs until the sugar is dissolved and whisk in the oil and applesauce. In another bowl combine the flour, baking powder, salt, and baking soda and stir the mixture into the sugar mixture alternately with the water. Stir in the bananas and walnuts, pour the batter into an oiled and floured large loaf pan, and bake the bread in a preheated 350° F. oven for about 1 hour. If the top browns too quickly, cover it with foil during the last 10 minutes of baking.

Makes 1 loaf.

Lemon Tea Loaf

Try a slice with a dollop of ice cream for dessert.

  $^1/_2$ C. butter
  1$^1/_2$ C. sugar
  2 large eggs
  1$^1/_2$ C. flour
  1 tsp. baking powder
  1 tsp. salt
  $^1/_2$ C. milk
  Juice and grated rind of 2 large lemons
  $^1/_2$ C. chopped walnuts (optional)

In the bowl of an electric mixer cream the butter with 1 cup sugar and beat in the eggs, one at time, beating after each addition. Into another bowl sift the flour, baking powder, and salt and beat the mixture into the egg mixture, one third at a time, alternately with the milk. Fold in the grated rind and nuts and scrape the batter into a greased 9- by 5-inch loaf pan. Bake the loaf in a preheated 350° F. oven for 1 hour.

In a saucepan combine the remaining $^1/_2$ cup sugar and the juice over low heat, stirring the mixture until the sugar is dissolved. Let the loaf stand for 5 minutes and slowly pour the sugar mixture over it. Let the loaf stand for 30 minutes and invert it onto a rack. Immediately turn the loaf upright.

Makes 1 loaf.

Pear and Pecan Bread

1 C. vegetable oil
2 C. sugar
3 large eggs
2½ C. peeled and finely chopped pears
    (about 3 large)
1 C. chopped pecans
2 tsp. vanilla
3 C. flour
½ tsp. salt
½ tsp. nutmeg
½ tsp. mace
1 tsp. baking soda
1 tsp. cinnamon

In a bowl combine the oil, sugar, and eggs, blending the mixture well. Stir in the pears, pecans, and vanilla. In another bowl combine the remaining ingredients and stir the dry ingredients into the pear mixture. Divide the batter between 2 greased loaf pans and bake the loaves in a preheated 350° F. oven for 1 hour, or until a wooden pick inserted in the center comes out clean. Let the loaves cool for 10 minutes and invert them onto racks to cool completely. Serve the bread with Raspberry Pear Butter (page 142).

Makes 2 loaves.

Cherry Pear Muffins

2 large eggs
½ C. vegetable oil
2 tsp. vanilla
2 lb. Bosc pears, peeled, cored, and finely
    chopped
1 C. sugar
2 C. flour
2 tsp. baking soda
2 tsp. cinnamon
½ tsp. nutmeg
½ tsp. mace
½ tsp. salt
¼ C. wheat germ
1 C. dried cherries
1 C. chopped pecans, toasted

In a large bowl whisk together the eggs, oil, and vanilla. In another bowl combine the pears and sugar and stir the mixture into the egg mixture. Sift the flour, baking soda, cinnamon, nutmeg, mace, and salt into a bowl and stir in the wheat germ. Stir the dry ingredients into the pear mixture and add the cherries and pecans, being careful not to overmix the batter. Spoon the batter into 18 well-greased muffin cups or foil or paper baking cups and bake the muffins in a preheated 325° F. oven for 30 minutes, or until they are lightly browned.

Makes 18 muffins.

Lemon and Ginger Muffins

A little tart, very gingery, and especially appealing with a cup of tea. Try making them as minis.

1/2 C. butter, softened
1 C. plus 2 T. sugar
2 large eggs
2 T. minced peeled gingerroot
2 T. grated lemon rind
1 tsp. baking soda
1 C. plain yogurt or buttermilk
1 C. flour
1/4 C. fresh lemon juice

In the large bowl of an electric mixer beat the butter and 1 cup sugar until the mixture is pale and fluffy. Beat in the eggs, one at a time, and add the ginger and lemon rind. Stir the baking soda into the yogurt. Alternately and one third at a time, fold the flour and the yogurt mixture into the butter mixture, combine the batter well, and spoon it into greased muffin cups or foil or paper baking cups. Bake the muffins in a preheated 375° F. oven for 18 to 20 minutes, or until they are lightly browned and springy to the touch.

In a small dish mix the lemon juice with the remaining sugar, stirring until the sugar dissolves.

Let the muffins cool for 3 to 5 minutes and dip each muffin into the juice mixture. Let the muffins cool completely on a rack.

Makes 12 muffins.

Many hours on Saturday mornings are spent by volunteers picking up and transporting goods and stacking the Center's shelves with the supplies needed for a week of distribution to our families.

Macadamia Nut Muffins

2 C. flour
1 C. plus 1 T. sugar
1/2 C. ground macadamia nuts
1/2 tsp. baking powder
1 1/4 sticks butter or margarine, cut into
  pieces
2 large eggs, lightly beaten
1 1/4 C. milk
1 1/4 C. macadamia nuts, toasted and
  chopped

In a large bowl combine the flour, sugar, ground macadamia nuts, and baking powder and with a pastry blender cut in the butter until the mixture resembles coarse meal. Add the eggs and milk and stir the mixture until it is just combined. Divide the batter among 12 buttered or lined muffin tins and sprinkle the tops with the chopped nuts. Bake the muffins in a preheated 400° F. oven for 10 minutes, reduce the heat to 350° F., and bake the muffins for 20 minutes more.

Makes 12 muffins.

Pecan Orange Muffins

Serve warm with a flavored butter or a dab of apple jelly and a slice of smoked turkey.

1 eating orange, well washed and dried
1/2 C. butter, softened
1 C. plus 1 T. sugar
2 large eggs
1 tsp. baking soda
2 C. flour
1 C. plain yogurt or buttermilk
3/4 C. finely chopped pecans

Finely grate the orange rind onto a sheet of wax paper, avoiding the white pith. Squeeze the orange to yield 1/3 cup orange juice.

In the bowl of an electric mixer beat the butter with 1 cup sugar until the mixture is pale and fluffy. Beat in the eggs, one at a time, and stir in the baking soda and grated rind. Alternately fold in half the flour and half the yogurt or buttermilk, repeat the process, and fold in the pecans. Spoon the batter into greased muffin cups or foil or paper baking cups and bake the muffins in a preheated 375° F. oven for 20 to 25 minutes, or until they are browned. Transfer the muffins to a rack and brush them with the orange juice. Sprinkle them with the remaining sugar and let them stand for 5 minutes before removing them from the pan.

Makes 12 muffins.

Pumpkin Chocolate Chip Muffins

Rich and spicy, delicious with espresso or cold milk, after school or before bed. The muffins can be wrapped in a plastic bag and kept for 2 to 3 days. They should be reheated before serving.

1²/₃ C. flour
1 C. sugar
1 T. pumpkin pie spice
1 tsp. baking soda
¹/₄ tsp. baking powder
¹/₄ tsp. salt
2 large eggs
1 C. canned pumpkin purée
¹/₂ C. butter, melted
1 C. chocolate chips
¹/₂ C. sliced unblanched almonds, toasted

In a large bowl whisk together the flour, sugar, pie spice, baking soda, baking powder, and salt.

In another bowl whisk together the eggs, pumpkin, and butter and stir in the chocolate chips and almonds. Fold the mixture into the dry ingredients until the batter is just combined and spoon it into greased muffin cups or foil or paper baking cups. Bake the muffins in a preheated 350° F. oven for 20 to 25 minutes, or until they are springy to the touch in the center. Transfer the muffins to a rack and let them cool.

Makes 12 regular muffins or 48 miniature muffins.

The Center holds parenting courses with discussions on such topics as child rearing, safety, family planning, and child discipline. They are led by social workers who volunteer their time.

Golden Raisin Rosemary Muffins

3/4 C. milk
1/2 C. golden raisins
1 tsp. finely crumbled rosemary
1/4 C. butter
1 1/2 C. flour
1/2 C. sugar
2 tsp. baking powder
1/4 tsp. salt
1 large egg

In a small saucepan combine the milk, raisins, and rosemary and simmer the mixture for 2 minutes. Remove the pan from the heat, add the butter, and stir the mixture until the butter is melted. Let the mixture cool.

In a bowl combine the flour, sugar, baking powder, and salt. Whisk the egg into the milk mixture and pour the mixture over the dry ingredients, blending the batter until it is just moistened. Spoon the batter into greased muffin cups or foil or paper baking cups and bake the muffins in a preheated 350° F. oven for 20 minutes, or until they are browned and springy to the touch in the center. Transfer the muffins to a rack and let them cool for 5 minutes. Invert them and serve them hot or at room temperature.

Makes 12 regular muffins or 24 miniatures.

Rhubarb Muffins

2 C. flour
1 T. baking powder
1/4 tsp. salt
1/4 tsp. cinnamon
1 large egg
1/2 C. packed light brown sugar
3 T. red currant jelly
1 C. milk
4 T. butter, melted
1/2 tsp. vanilla
1 1/2 C. diced rhubarb, or 2 C. frozen diced rhubarb, thawed

In a large bowl combine the flour, baking powder, salt, and cinnamon. In another bowl whisk together the egg, sugar, and jelly until the mixture is smooth (the jelly will not completely dissolve) and whisk in the milk, butter, and vanilla. Stir in the rhubarb. Pour the mixture over the dry ingredients and fold the batter together until it is just blended. Spoon the batter into greased muffin cups or foil or paper baking cups and bake the muffins in a preheated 375° F. oven for 20 to 30 minutes, or until they are light brown and springy to the touch in the center. Transfer the muffins to a rack and let them cool for at least 15 minutes before serving. Serve the muffins topped with Very Strawberry Butter (page 142).

Makes 14 muffins.

Picnic Torte

Terrific at a tailgating or beach party.

2 loaves frozen bread dough, thawed
1 T. chopped fresh thyme or 1 tsp. dried
1 red onion, chopped
1 garlic clove, minced
3 C. sliced mushrooms
4 T. extra virgin olive oil
Salt and pepper to taste
4 zucchini, thinly sliced
1/2 lb. fresh spinach leaves, trimmed of coarse
  stems
2/3 C. shredded Monterey Jack cheese
2/3 C. shredded mozzarella cheese
8 oz. pepperoni, thinly sliced

Combine the bread dough and let it rise until it is double in bulk. On a floured board roll the dough into a 20-inch circle and sprinkle it with the thyme. Transfer it to a greased 10-inch springform pan, letting the edges drape over the sides.

In a skillet sauté the onion, garlic, and mushrooms in 2 tablespoons of the oil for about 5 minutes, or until the onion is softened. Add the salt and pepper and transfer the mixture to a plate. Add 1 tablespoon oil to the pan and sauté the zucchini until it is softened. Layer half the mushroom mixture, half the zucchini, half the spinach, half of each of the cheeses, and half the pepperoni in the springform pan and repeat the layering. Bring the dough together over the top of the vegetables, leaving a small steam vent, and brush the dough lightly with the remaining oil. Bake the torte in a preheated 375° F. oven for 50 minutes, or until the top is golden brown and crusty. Serve the torte warm or at room temperature.

Serves 10 to 12.

Under certain circumstances there are few hours in life more agreeable than the hour dedicated to the ceremony known as afternoon tea.

Henry James (1843–1916),
U.S. author

Spinach, Feta, and Caramelized Onion Pizza

1 recipe Pizza Dough (page 136)
2 large onions, sliced into rings
3 T. extra virgin olive oil
1 tsp. sugar
1 (10-oz.) package frozen chopped spinach, thawed and squeezed dry
3/4 C. tomato sauce
1/2 lb. Feta cheese, crumbled
4 oz. mozzarella cheese, grated
1/3 C. chopped walnuts
Nutmeg and freshly ground pepper to taste

Make Pizza Dough.

In a skillet sauté the onions in 2 tablespoons of the olive oil, stirring, over moderately high heat for 5 minutes. Reduce the heat to moderately low, sprinkle the onions with the sugar, and cook them over low heat, stirring occasionally, for 10 to 15 minutes more, or until they are very brown. Add the spinach and cook the mixture for about 3 minutes, breaking up the spinach and combining it with the onions. Let the mixture partially cool.

Spread the tomato sauce to within 1/2 inch of the edge of the pizza dough and drizzle the remaining tablespoon of olive oil over it. Spread the spinach and onion mixture evenly over the sauce and sprinkle it with the Feta cheese, mozzarella, and walnuts. Sprinkle the top with the nutmeg and pepper and bake the pizza in a preheated 450° F. oven for 12 to 15 minutes, or until the cheese is melted and the edge of the crust is beginning to brown. To serve as an hors d'oeuvre bake it in a rectangular shape and cut it into 1- by 3-inch pieces. For easiest cutting, use a pizza wheel.

Makes one 14-inch round pizza.

Pizza Mediterranée

1 recipe Pizza Dough (page 136)
1 red onion, sliced
1 1/2 C. arugula
2/3 C. chopped sun-dried tomatoes
3 oz. minced prosciutto
4 oz. Fontina cheese, grated
1/4 C. pine nuts, toasted
1 C. shredded mozzarella

Make Pizza Dough.

Spread the onion and arugula evenly on the dough and top them with the remaining ingredients. Bake the pizza in a preheated 450° F. oven for 12 to 15 minutes, or until the cheese is melted and the edge of the crust is lightly browned.

Makes one 14-inch round pizza.

Three-Bean Pizza

1 large onion, coarsely chopped
1 T. extra virgin olive oil
3 garlic cloves, minced
1 (15-oz.) can black beans, drained and rinsed
1 (8-oz.) can red kidney beans, drained and rinsed
1 (8-oz.) can chick-peas, drained and rinsed
1 (12-oz.) jar chunky salsa
1/4 C. chopped cilantro
1 prepared pizza crust, baked
1 C. shredded Monterey Jack cheese

In a large skillet sauté the onion in the olive oil over moderately high heat for 3 minutes, or until it is softened. Add the garlic and sauté the mixture for 2 minutes. Add the beans, chick-peas, salsa, and cilantro and cook the mixture, stirring occasionally, for about 5 minutes, or until it is heated through. Sprinkle the crust with half the cheese, spoon the bean mixture over the cheese, spreading it evenly, and sprinkle it with the remaining cheese. Bake the pizza in a preheated 425° F. oven for 10 minutes, or until it is hot and bubbly.

Makes one 14-inch round pizza.

Cheeses can be flavored in many ways by herbs. Goat cheese, because of its characteristic mildness, is enhanced by the flavor of fresh herbs, along with garlic, black pepper, and a spoonful or two of white wine.

Pizza Dough

1 to 1½ C. warm water
1 package dry yeast
¼ tsp. sugar
3 to 3⅓ C. unbleached all-purpose flour (or
    substitute 1 cup whole wheat flour for 1
    cup of the all-purpose flour)
2 tsp. oregano
1 tsp. basil
1 tsp. salt
2 tsp. fennel seed
Freshly ground black pepper to taste
2 T. extra virgin olive oil

In a measuring cup pour the yeast into 1 cup warm water and stir in the sugar. Let the mixture stand until the yeast becomes bubbly. In a food processor combine the flour, oregano, basil, salt, fennel seed, and pepper and process the mixture until it is combined. With the motor running pour the yeast mixture and the oil through the feed tube and continue to process the mixture for about 2 minutes, or until it forms a ball of very soft slightly sticky dough. If the dough is too hard, add more warm water, 1 tablespoon at a time, processing the dough well after each addition, until it is very soft and slightly sticky. Transfer the dough to a greased bowl, turn it to coat both sides with grease, and let it rise in a warm place, covered with a sheet of plastic wrap, for 1 to 2 hours, or until it is double in bulk.

Punch down the dough, turn it out onto a large clean flat surface, and with a rolling pin roll it into a large circle or rectangle to fit into a greased pizza pan or jelly-roll pan. (The dough will be very elastic and difficult to roll, so it may be necessary to push it out into the desired shape with your hands.) Fit the dough into the pan and let it rise again, covered lightly with plastic wrap, for about 30 minutes. (The dough may be allowed to rise for 1 to 1½ hours longer if a puffier crust is desired.)

Makes enough dough for one 14-inch round pizza.

Scrambled Eggs with Chive, Smoked Trout, and Tomatoes

A stunning presentation. Smoked salmon may be substituted for the trout.

4 tomatoes, halved
Salt and pepper to taste
12 large eggs
1/3 C. half-and-half
1/4 C. butter
2 T. chopped chive or scallion
1 lb. smoked trout, skinned, boned, flaked, and
    cut into small pieces

On a buttered baking sheet arrange the tomatoes, cut sides up, and broil them 6 inches from a preheated broiler for about 5 minutes, or until they are lightly colored and tender, watching them closely to avoid burning. Season the tomatoes with salt and pepper and tent them with foil to keep them warm.

In a bowl whisk together the eggs, half-and-half, and salt and pepper. In a large nonstick skillet melt the butter over low heat and in it cook the eggs, stirring frequently, for about 6 minutes, or until they are almost set. Stir in the chive and remove the pan from the heat. Spoon the eggs onto a platter, sprinkle them with the trout, and arrange the tomatoes around the edge.

Serves 6 to 8.

Don't save all your smiles for the parlor – use a few in the kitchen.

Cranberry Coffee Cake

A wonderful, refreshing morning surprise, which, made ahead, can be frozen and reheated. The glaze is best applied after reheating.

- 1/2 C. butter, softened
- 1 C. sugar
- 2 large eggs
- 2 C. flour
- 1 tsp. baking powder
- 1/2 tsp. salt
- 1 tsp. baking soda
- 1 C. sour cream
- 1 tsp. vanilla
- 1 1/4 C. whole cranberry sauce
- 1/3 C. chopped pecans

In the bowl of an electric mixer cream the butter and sugar until the mixture is light and add the eggs, one at a time, beating well after each addition. Into a bowl sift together the flour, baking powder, salt, and baking soda and add the mixture to the butter mixture, one-third at a time, alternately with the sour cream and vanilla.

Transfer half the batter to an oiled 8-inch tube pan or bundt pan and spoon the cranberry sauce over it. Top the sauce with the remaining batter, swirl the batter slightly, and bake the cake in a preheated 350° F. oven for 45 to 55 minutes, or until it just begins to pull away from the sides of the pan. Let the cake cool on a rack for 10 minutes and invert it onto the rack. Turn the cake right side up and drizzle it with the glaze or dust it with confectioners' sugar. Sprinkle the top with the pecans.

Serves 10.

Glaze

- 1/2 C. confectioners' sugar
- 2 to 2 1/2 tsp. warm water
- 1/2 tsp. vanilla or almond flavoring

In a bowl combine the sugar, water, and flavoring until the mixture is smooth.

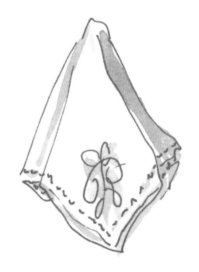

Grilled Apple and Pear Sandwich

6 T. butter or margarine
1 large apple, cored and thinly sliced
1 large pear, cored and thinly sliced
1/2 C. chutney
1/2 C. chopped walnuts
1/2 lb. Cheddar cheese, thinly sliced
1/4 lb. blue cheese, crumbled
8 thick slices country-style bread

In a large skillet melt 4 tablespoons of the butter, add the apple and pear, and cook the fruits over high heat, stirring, for 5 minutes, or until they are tender and most of the juices have evaporated. Stir in the chutney and walnuts and remove the pan from the heat. Arrange the Cheddar cheese on 4 slices of bread and divide the fruit mixture over it. Sprinkle each serving with blue cheese and top the sandwiches with the remaining bread. Melt the remaining butter in the skillet and in it brown the sandwiches on both sides.

Serves 4.

*Drink tea and forget
the world's noises.*

*The mere chink of cups
and saucers tunes the mind
to happy repose.*

French Toast with Apples

What a delectable way to begin a day!

1 C. dark brown sugar
1/2 C. butter
1 tsp. cinnamon
2 T. light corn syrup
2 tart apples, peeled, cored, and sliced
5 large eggs
1 1/2 C. milk
1 tsp. vanilla
1 loaf French bread, cut into 3/4-inch slices

In a saucepan cook the sugar, butter, cinnamon, and syrup until the mixture is syrupy and pour it into a 9 x 13-inch baking dish. Spread the apple slices over the syrup and arrange the bread over the apples. In a bowl whisk together the remaining ingredients and pour the mixture over the bread. Chill the dish, covered, overnight. Bake the dish in a preheated 350° F. oven for 45 minutes and serve it with maple syrup, if desired.

Serves 6 to 8.

French Breakfast Puffs

This gets a little messy during the dipping, but guests and family will be very grateful for the results.

1 C. sugar
1 tsp. cinnamon
1/3 C. solid shortening
1 large egg
1 1/2 C. flour
1 1/2 tsp. baking powder
1/2 tsp. salt
1/4 tsp. nutmeg
1/2 C. whole milk
1/2 C. butter or margarine, melted

In a small dish combine 1/2 cup sugar and the cinnamon and reserve the mixture. In the bowl of an electric mixer combine the shortening, the remaining sugar, and the egg and beat the mixture until it is smooth. In another bowl combine the flour, baking powder, salt, and nutmeg and stir the mixture into the egg mixture alternately with the milk. Pour the batter into 12 well-greased muffin tins, filling each half full, and bake the puffs in a preheated 350° F. oven for 20 to 25 minutes.

Immediately remove the puffs from the tins and roll them in the melted butter. Roll them next in the reserved cinnamon sugar and serve them immediately.

Makes 12 puffs.

Whole Grain Pancakes

A glorious morning treat! Try gilding the pancakes with homemade applesauce or vanilla yogurt and fresh berries.

2/3 C. uncooked oatmeal
11/3 C. whole wheat flour
2/3 C. yellow cornmeal
2/3 C. flour
4 tsp. baking powder
2 tsp. baking soda
2 tsp. salt
11/2 sticks butter, sliced
31/2 C. buttermilk plus additional buttermilk or
    milk, if needed
4 large eggs
1/3 C. maple syrup

In a food processor grind the oatmeal to a powder, add the remaining dry ingredients, and combine the mixture. Add the butter and process the mixture until it is the consistency of cornmeal. In a bowl combine the buttermilk, eggs, and syrup, add the mixture to the dry ingredients and process the batter, turning the machine on and off, until it is just combined. Add more buttermilk if the batter is too thick. Cook the pancakes on a hot griddle, turning them once, until they are golden brown.

Serves 8 to 10.

It still holds true that man is most uniquely human when he turns obstacles into opportunities.

Eric Hoffer (1902–1983),
U.S. philosopher

Raspberry Pear Butter

   2 lb. firm ripe Bosc pears, cored and cut
      into large chunks
   1 C. fresh or frozen raspberries
   1½ T. sugar

In a food processor chop the pears coarsely
and transfer them to a saucepan. In the food
processor purée the raspberries and add them to
the pan, or, if a smoother butter is desired, strain
them into the pan. Add the sugar and bring the
mixture to a boil, stirring. Reduce the heat to
moderately low and cook the mixture, stirring
occasionally, for about 1½ hours, or until it is very
thick and most of the juice has evaporated. Let the
butter cool and transfer it to a crock or jar.

Makes about 2 cups.

Very Strawberry Butter

   4 T. unsalted butter, softened
   2 to 2½ T. strawberry preserves

In a small bowl beat the butter with a wooden
spoon until it is almost the consistency of sour
cream. Beat in the preserves, 1 tablespoon at a time,
and store the butter tightly covered and chilled.
Serve it at room temperature.

Makes about ½ cup.

Herb Butter

   ½ C. butter, softened
   2 to 4 T. minced parsley
   1 to 2 T. minced mixed herbs, such as dill,
      savory, thyme, oregano, or chives
   Salt and pepper to taste

In a small bowl beat the butter with a wooden
spoon until it is very soft, beat in 2 tablespoons of
the parsley and 2 teaspoons of the mixed herbs.
Add more herbs to taste and the salt and pepper.
Store the butter tightly covered and chilled.

Makes about ⅔ cup.

Honey Butter

   4 T. unsalted butter, softened
   1 T. honey, such as sourwood or buckwheat

In a small bowl beat the butter and honey until
it is fluffy and well mixed. Store the butter tightly
covered. It will keep indefinitely in the refrigerator.

Makes about ⅓ cup.

Sweets

Sweets

Apple Cheddar Crumble

2 lb. tart green apples, peeled, cored, and
    sliced
1/2 C. golden raisins
1 C. firmly packed light brown sugar
2 tsp. cinnamon
1 tsp. nutmeg
1/4 tsp. ground cardamom
2/3 C. flour
1 1/4 C. finely shredded sharp Cheddar
    cheese, at room temperature (not
    packaged shredded cheese)
4 T. cold unsalted butter, cut into 1-inch
    pieces
2/3 C. coarsely chopped pecans

In a bowl combine the apples, raisins, 2/3 cup of the brown sugar, and the spices and transfer the mixture to a buttered shallow 3-quart baking dish. In a small bowl combine the remaining sugar, the flour, and 3/4 cup of the cheese. Cut in the butter with a pastry blender until the mixture resembles coarse crumbs and stir in the remaining cheese and pecans. Sprinkle the mixture over the apples and bake the crumble in a preheated 400° F. oven for 35 to 40 minutes, or until the apples are tender and the topping is golden. Let the crumble stand for 5 minutes. Spoon the crumble into a bowl and serve it hot or warm with Crème Anglaise or ice cream.

Serves 6.

Crème Anglaise

6 egg yolks
1/2 C. sugar
2 C. milk
2 tsp. vanilla

Fill a large bowl with ice cubes and cold water and reserve it.

In a bowl beat together the egg yolks and sugar, add the milk, and strain the mixture into the top of a double boiler. Cook the custard over simmering water, stirring constantly, for 15 to 20 minutes, or until it is thickened and coats the spoon. Remove the pan from the heat, continuing to stir, and set the pan in the bowl of ice water. Stir the mixture until it is cool, add the vanilla, and transfer the sauce to a pitcher or bowl. Serve the sauce immediately or chill it, covered, until serving time.

Makes about 2 1/2 cups.

Gingered Grapefruit Baskets

6 pink grapefruit
2 to 3 pts. vanilla ice cream or frozen yogurt
1/3 C. firmly packed light brown sugar
4 1/2 tsp. minced peeled gingerroot or
    crystallized ginger
6 sprigs of mint

Halve the grapefruit horizontally and cut around each half and between the segments to release the segments. Put the segments into a bowl, discarding the seeds, and remove all the membranes from 6 of the halves, discarding the remaining halves.

Put a large scoop of ice cream or yogurt into each grapefruit half and keep the halves in the freezer, covered, until just before serving.

Add the sugar and ginger to the grapefruit segments, toss the mixture gently, and chill it, covered, for at least 2 hours, or overnight.

Spoon some of the grapefruit mixture over the ice cream in each grapefruit half and garnish each serving with a sprig of mint. Pass the remaining grapefruit mixture separately.

Serves 6.

Caramel Poached Pears

These pears make a wonderful autumn dessert, especially accompanied by a crisp nut-strewn cookie. They are also delicious cold, although the syrup must be reblended. They can be reheated – gently – in the microwave.

1/3 C. light corn syrup
1/3 C. dark brown sugar
1 tsp. vanilla
6 Bosc or Anjou pears, peeled, cored, and
    halved lengthwise
1/3 C. heavy cream
Whipped cream or *crème fraîche* for garnish

In a small saucepan combine the corn syrup and sugar and cook the mixture over moderately low heat for 2 minutes, or until the sugar has dissolved. Stir in the vanilla and arrange the pears in a buttered baking dish just large enough to hold them in one layer. Pour the syrup over them and bake them, covered with a sheet of foil, in a preheated 375° F. oven for 30 minutes. Baste the pears with the syrup and continue to bake them, uncovered, for 30 minutes more, basting two more times. Transfer the pears without the syrup to a serving dish and pour the syrup into the saucepan. Cook the syrup until it begins to thicken and gradually stir in the heavy cream. Cook the sauce over moderate heat for 2 minutes more and pour it over the pears. Serve the pears warm with whipped cream or *crème fraîche.*

Serves 6.

Spiced Blueberry and Maple Cornmeal Cobbler

4 C. blueberries
1 C. plus 2 T. granulated sugar
1 T. quick tapioca
2 tsp. grated lemon rind
1 tsp. cinnamon
$\frac{1}{2}$ tsp. nutmeg
1 C. flour
$\frac{1}{2}$ C. cornmeal
2 tsp. baking powder
$\frac{1}{2}$ tsp. baking soda
$\frac{1}{2}$ tsp. salt
$\frac{1}{2}$ C. plus 2 T. unsalted butter
1 C. confectioners' sugar
1 large egg
$\frac{3}{4}$ C. buttermilk
2 T. maple syrup
Sweetened whipped cream or ice cream

In a buttered 10-inch shallow baking dish combine the blueberries, granulated sugar, tapioca, lemon rind, cinnamon, and nutmeg. In a bowl combine the flour, cornmeal, baking powder, baking soda, and salt. In another bowl cream the $\frac{1}{2}$ cup butter with the confectioners' sugar until the mixture is light and fluffy and beat in the egg and buttermilk. Stir in the flour mixture and pour the batter over the berry mixture. Bake the cobbler in a preheated 375° F. oven for 35 to 40 minutes, or until it is bubbly and the topping springs back lightly when touched. Remove the dish from the oven and change the oven setting to "broil."

In a dish combine the remaining butter, melted, with the syrup and brush the mixture on the cobbler. Broil the cobbler for about 1 minute, or until the top is lightly glazed. Serve the cobbler warm with sweetened whipped cream or ice cream.

Serves 6 to 8.

Some of our very active volunteers are senior citizens. They perform a variety of jobs including record keeping, correspondence, and interviewing prospective families.

White Chocolate Mousse Cake

A recipe from the Simon Pearce Restaurant

8 oz. chocolate wafers
6 T. butter, melted
1 lb. white chocolate
4 large eggs
Pinch of salt
3/4 C. sugar
3 C. heavy cream
2 1/2 T. white *crème de cacao*

Butter the sides only of a 10-inch springform pan. In a food processor crush the wafers until the crumbs are very fine and combine them with the butter. Press about two thirds of the crumbs onto the sides of the pan and spread the remaining crumbs evenly in the bottom of the pan, pressing them in with the bottom of a glass. Bake the crust in a preheated 350° F. oven for 5 minutes and transfer it to a rack to cool completely. Put the pan in the freezer until the mousse is ready.

In a double boiler over simmering water melt the chocolate, stirring it with a whisk until it is smooth. Separate the eggs, putting the whites in a large bowl and the yolks in another large bowl. Beat the whites with an electric mixer until they are frothy, add the salt, and gradually beat in the sugar, continuing to beat the meringue until it is thick and glossy.

Whisk the chocolate into the egg yolks, whisking until the mixture is well combined, and whisk in a bit of heavy cream, if necessary, to smooth the mixture. Stir in the *crème de cacao*. Fold the meringue gently into the yolk mixture until it is well combined.

In the mixer beat the cream until it holds soft peaks and fold it into the chocolate mixture. Pour the mousse into the prepared shell and freeze the cake for at least 4 hours, or overnight.

Serve the cake with Lemon Raspberry Sauce.

Serves 12.

Lemon Raspberry Sauce

12 oz. frozen raspberries
Sugar to taste
Juice of 1 lemon

In a food processor purée the raspberries with the sugar and lemon juice and strain the mixture through a fine sieve into a bowl.

Makes about 1 1/2 cups.

Peach and Macaroon Mousse

The amount of cream can be reduced for a denser mousse. Strained puréed raspberries make a heavenly – and very pretty – topping for this great do-ahead dessert.

6 large ripe peaches, peeled and quartered
1 T. lemon juice
1 C. sugar
1 C. dry macaroon crumbs, preferably made from very dry Italian macaroons, plus extra for garnish
3 T. kirsch
Pinch of salt
2½ C. heavy cream, whipped until it holds soft peaks

In a food processor purée the peaches and in a large bowl combine the purée with the lemon juice, sugar, crumbs, kirsch, and salt. Fold in the cream and freeze the mixture until it is just mushy. Beat the mixture with a spoon until it is of an even consistency, pour it into a decorative freezer-proof bowl, and freeze it until it is firm. Serve the mousse sprinkled with additional macaroon crumbs.

Serves 6.

Our oldest volunteer is eighty-two, our youngest is fifteen – proof that one is never too old or too young to help others.

Scandinavian Apple Bread Pudding

6 T. butter
2½ C. finely ground white bread crumbs,
    from homemade-type bread
4 C. homemade-type applesauce
1 C. seedless black raspberry jam
Lightly sweetened whipped cream for
    garnish

In a skillet melt the butter and in it cook the crumbs over moderate heat, stirring, for 4 to 5 minutes, or until they are golden. Spread 1 cup of the crumbs in the bottom of a buttered 1½-quart round baking dish and top the crumbs with half the applesauce. Spread ½ cup jam over the applesauce and repeat the layering. Sprinkle the remaining crumbs on top and bake the pudding in a preheated 325° F. oven for 25 minutes, or until it is lightly browned. Serve the pudding warm accompanied by the whipped cream.

Serves 6.

Brandied Apricot Cobbler

¾ C. plus 1 T. sugar
1 T. cornstarch
¼ C. Cognac
1 T. lemon juice
½ tsp. grated lemon rind
½ tsp. nutmeg
2 lb. apricots, pitted and sliced
1½ C. cake flour
1½ tsp. baking powder
¼ tsp. salt
4 T. cold unsalted butter, cut into pieces
2 egg yolks or 3 egg whites
⅓ C. sour cream

In a 2- or 3-quart greased baking dish combine 4 tablespoons of the sugar, the cornstarch, Cognac, lemon juice, lemon rind, and nutmeg, add the apricots, and toss the mixture. In a large bowl combine the remaining ½ cup sugar, the flour, baking powder, and salt and cut in the butter with a pastry blender until the mixture resembles coarse crumbs.

In a bowl beat the egg yolks or whites and sour cream until the mixture is blended, pour the mixture over the flour mixture, and stir the batter with a fork until it is just blended. Drop spoonfuls of the batter over the apricots, sprinkle the cobbler with the remaining tablespoon of sugar, and bake it in a preheated 400° F. oven for 30 to 35 minutes, or until the topping is golden brown and the filling is bubbling. Let the cobbler cool for 10 minutes before serving.

Serves 6.

Lemon Walnut Tart

1 (9-inch) pie crust, made from Sweet Pastry
　　Dough (page 169), baked
²/₃ C. light corn syrup
6 T. butter, softened
²/₃ C. packed brown sugar
3 large eggs
¹/₄ C. lemon juice
2 T. white cornmeal
2 tsp. grated lemon rind
1¹/₂ C. chopped walnuts
Lightly sweetened whipped cream

In a bowl combine the corn syrup, butter, brown sugar, eggs, lemon juice, cornmeal, and lemon rind, beat the mixture until it is smooth, and stir in the walnuts. Pour the filling into the shell and bake the tart in a preheated 375° F. oven for 40 to 45 minutes, or until the filling is almost, but not quite, set. Let the tart cool on a rack for at least 30 minutes and serve it warm or at room temperature with lightly sweetened whipped cream.

Serves 6 to 8.

No flowers for a table centerpiece? Try using almost any small collection — mugs, porcelain animals, candlesticks, bells, books, cups and saucers, vases, old brass or silver, unusual perfume bottles — the list is endless.

Ricotta Tart with Chocolate and Raspberry Sauces

A recipe from Chef Jim Lupia

1 (9-inch) pastry shell, made from Sweet
   Pastry Dough (page 169), baked
1¼ C. ricotta cheese, or low-fat ricotta
3 large eggs, separated
¼ C. sugar
1 tsp. vanilla
Optional: 2 T. liqueur, such as Kahlúa or
   Tia Maria, added to the ricotta mixture
Optional: 4 oz. semisweet chocolate, melted,
   added to the ricotta mixture

In a large bowl combine the ricotta, egg yolks, sugar, and vanilla and blend the mixture well. In another bowl beat the egg whites until they hold stiff moist peaks and gently fold them into the ricotta mixture. Spoon the filling into the crust, smoothing the top, and bake the tart in a preheated 350° F. oven for about 45 minutes, or until it is just golden. Let the tart cool completely on a wire rack, transfer it to a platter, and serve it at room temperature with Chocolate Sauce and Raspberry Sauce.

Serves 12.

Chocolate Sauce

8 oz. semisweet chocolate, chopped
2 T. unsalted butter
1 C. heavy cream
1 tsp. vanilla

In a saucepan combine the chocolate, butter, and cream and cook the mixture over low heat, stirring frequently, until the chocolate is melted and the mixture is smooth. Or, in a microwave-safe bowl melt and blend the mixture in the microwave on medium power, stirring frequently. Remove the pan from the heat and stir in the vanilla. This sauce may be made 24 hours ahead and kept, chilled and covered.

Makes about 1½ cups.

Raspberry Sauce

1 (12-oz.) package frozen raspberries,
   thawed
¼ C. currant jelly
2 T. sugar
2 T. cassis

Press the berries through a strainer to remove the seeds. In a saucepan combine the purée, jelly, and sugar and bring the mixture to a boil. Cook the mixture until it is reduced by half and let it cool. Stir in the cassis and chill the sauce, covered.

Makes about 1½ cups.

Weybridge Linzer Torte

²/₃ C. skinned hazelnuts
2 sticks butter, softened
1 C. sugar
1 T. grated orange rind
1 T. grated lemon rind
2 egg yolks
1¹/₂ C. sifted flour
2 tsp. cinnamon
1 tsp. baking powder
¹/₂ tsp. ground clove
¹/₄ tsp. salt
¹/₂ C. seedless raspberry jam
¹/₂ C. currant jelly
Confectioners' sugar to taste

In a food processor grind the nuts fine.

In an electric mixer bowl combine the butter and sugar and beat the mixture until it is fluffy. Beat in the orange and lemon rinds and add the eggs yolks, one at a time, beating after each addition.

Into a bowl sift the flour, cinnamon, baking powder, clove, and salt and stir the mixture into the butter mixture, combining the mixture well. Stir in the ground nuts and chill the dough for at least 2 hours.

Separate and reserve one third of the dough, chilled. Press the remaining dough into the bottom of a 9-inch springform pan. In a small bowl combine the jam and jelly and spread the mixture over the dough. On a floured board roll the reserved dough into a 9-inch round and with a floured knife cut it into ¹/₂-inch strips. Arrange the strips over the jam mixture lattice fashion, patching any strips that break with scraps of dough. Bake the torte in a preheated 350° F. oven for 50 minutes, or until the strips are lightly browned. Transfer the torte to a rack and remove the sides of the pan. Sprinkle the top with the confectioners' sugar and serve the torte in thin wedges.

Serves 10 to 12.

Make chocolate mint leaves by brushing melted chocolate on fresh mint leaves and then peeling away the actual leaves when the chocolate has hardened.

Honey Pecan Torte with Chocolate Glaze

A luscious and very rich dessert — serve in small pieces. This torte is wonderful to have on hand at holiday time because it can be kept, in the refrigerator, for 2 to 3 weeks.

> 1½ recipes Sweet Pastry Dough (page 169)
> 1 C. sugar
> 2½ oz. water
> 2⅓ C. chopped pecans
> 1 stick plus 1 T. butter
> ½ C. milk
> ¼ C. honey
> 1 T. chopped pecans for decoration

On a floured board roll out two thirds of the dough into a 9- or 10-inch round, depending on whether you are using an 8- or 9-inch tart pan, and fit the dough into the pan. Trim away and reserve the excess dough and chill the shell, the reserved dough, and the remaining third for 1 hour.

In a heavy skillet combine the sugar and water and cook the syrup over moderately low heat until the sugar has dissolved. Increase the heat to high and cook the syrup, stirring occasionally and swirling the pan, until the syrup is a light caramel color. Remove the pan from the heat and stir in the 2⅓ cups pecans, butter, and milk. Return the pan to low heat and simmer the mixture for 15 minutes. Stir in the honey.

Combine the remaining third of the dough and the reserved dough and roll it into a round the diameter of the pan. Pour the filling into the shell, arrange the round of dough over it, trimming any overhanging edges, and press the round into the dough around the edges to seal the torte. Cut a slit in the top and bake the torte in a preheated 425° F. oven for 20 minutes, or until it is browned. Let the torte cool for 4 hours and invert it onto a serving dish.

Spread the top and sides of the torte with Chocolate Glaze and decorate the top with the 1 tablespoon chopped pecans.

Chocolate Glaze

> 4 oz. semisweet chocolate
> 2½ T. butter, softened
> ½ tsp. vegetable oil

In the microwave, or in the top of a double boiler, combine the chocolate, butter, and oil and heat the mixture, stirring, until the chocolate is melted and the mixture is smooth.

Serves 12 to 14.

Blueberry Cheese Tart

1 (9-inch) pie crust, made from Sweet Pastry
    Dough (page 169), baked
8 oz. low-fat cream cheese
3/4 C. sugar
1½ tsp. grated lemon rind
2 large eggs
1 T. flour
1¾ C. blueberries

In a food processor whip the cheese until it is
smooth, add the sugar, lemon rind, eggs, and flour, and
beat the mixture until it is well combined and the sugar is
dissolved. Spread the berries in the shell, pour the cheese
mixture over them, and bake the tart in a preheated
350° F. oven for 30 minutes, or until the filling is set. Let
the tart cool on a rack.

Serves 8.

*Mint leaves are a most
appealing garnish. To dress
them up a bit, crystallize
them by dipping them
first in beaten egg white
and then in sugar.*

Tennessee Carrot Cake

This is a voluptuous, satisfying cake, which remains moist and keeps well (if hidden!) for several days.

2 C. flour
1 tsp. baking powder
1 tsp. baking soda
1 tsp. salt
1½ tsp. cinnamon
½ tsp. allspice
1¾ C. sugar
4 large eggs
1½ C. vegetable oil
½ tsp. vanilla
2 T. sour cream
2 C. grated carrot (2½ to 3 large carrots)
1 C. grated apple
½ C. currants
½ C. chopped walnuts or pecans

In a bowl whisk together the flour, baking powder, baking soda, salt, cinnamon, and allspice. In another bowl beat the sugar with the eggs until the sugar is dissolved and the mixture is light. Add the oil in a thin stream, beating, and the sour cream and vanilla and stir in the flour mixture, combining the batter well. Fold in the carrot, apple, currants, and nuts and transfer the batter to the pans. Bake the cake in a preheated 350° F. oven for 40 minutes, or until the tops spring back when pressed lightly with a finger. Let the rounds cool on racks for 5 minutes and invert them onto the racks to cool completely. Peel off and discard the wax papers. Ice the layers with Cream Cheese Frosting.

Serves 10 to 12.

Cream Cheese Frosting

10 oz. reduced-fat cream cheese, softened
2 T. butter, softened
3 C. confectioners' sugar
1 tsp. vanilla
Orange-flavored liqueur to taste, if desired

In the bowl of an electric mixer combine the cream cheese and butter and gradually beat in the sugar. Add the vanilla and liqueur, if desired, and continue to beat the frosting until it is smooth. If the frosting becomes dry while icing the cake, beat in a few drops of warm water.

Makes enough to generously ice the tops and sides of two 9- or 10-inch layers.

Almond Bundt Cake

1/2 lb. almond paste
11/4 C. sugar
1 C. unsalted butter, softened
5 large eggs
1 C. sour cream
2 tsp. vanilla
1 tsp. almond extract
3 C. flour
11/2 tsp. baking powder
1 tsp. baking soda

In a food processor combine the almond paste and the sugar and blend the mixture until it is well combined. Add the butter and continue to process the mixture. Add the eggs, one at a time, and blend in the sour cream and flavorings.

In a bowl sift together the flour, baking powder, and soda and add it to the batter, one third at a time. Transfer the batter to a buttered and floured bundt pan and bake the cake in the middle of a preheated 325° F. oven for about 1 hour, or until it is springy to the touch. Let the cake cool on a rack for 10 minutes and invert it onto a serving plate. This cake will keep well, tightly wrapped.

Serves 10 to 12.

Edible flowers make delightful garnishes for many foods, especially salads and desserts. A few of the most enticing are: Wild Chicory, Violet, Calendula, Woodruff, Carnation, Squash Blossom, Clover, Rosemary, Chive Blossom, Rose, Daisy, Day Lily, Orange Blossom, Nasturtium, Lemon Bergamot and Lavender.

Zucchini Chocolate Cake with Orange Glaze

A terrific dessert for an outdoor party because it travels well.

2 C. sliced zucchini (2 or 3 medium)
1/2 C. orange juice
3/4 tsp. salt
2 C. flour
1 tsp. baking powder
1 tsp. baking soda
1 tsp. cinnamon
1/2 tsp. nutmeg
1/4 C. unsweetened cocoa
3 large eggs
2 C. sugar
1/2 C. vegetable oil
3/4 C. buttermilk
1 tsp. vanilla
1 tsp. grated orange rind
1 C. coarsely chopped pecans or walnuts, toasted

In a saucepan combine the zucchini with the orange juice and 1/2 teaspoon salt and cook it over moderate heat for about 10 minutes, or until it is tender. Purée the zucchini in a blender or food processor and reserve it.

Sift the flour, baking powder, baking soda, cinnamon, nutmeg, cocoa, and remaining salt into a bowl. In the bowl of an electric mixer beat the eggs until they are creamy and beat in the sugar, beating the mixture until it is very light. Gradually beat in the oil and continue to beat the batter until it is fluffy and very pale.

Stir the buttermilk into the reserved zucchini and add the mixture alternately with the dry ingredients to the egg mixture, combining the batter at low speed until it is well incorporated. Stir in the vanilla, orange rind, and nuts and pour the batter into a greased and floured 13- by 9- by 2-inch baking pan. Bake the cake in a preheated 350° F. oven for 40 to 50 minutes, or until a cake tester comes out clean. Let the cake cool on a rack for 10 minutes and invert it onto the rack to cool completely. Drizzle the cake with Orange Glaze.

Serves 12.

Orange Glaze

1 C. confectioners' sugar
1/4 C. orange juice
1 tsp. grated orange rind
1 T. butter, melted and hot

In a small bowl combine all the ingredients until the glaze is smooth.

Fabulous Skillet Toffee

Unfortunately, this recipe cannot be doubled – but it's so quick to make that you can easily do two batches in succession. Include it in gifts of Christmas cookies.

    1 C. sugar
    2 sticks butter
    3 T. water
    1 T. light corn syrup
    5 oz. sliced almonds
    8 oz. Hershey's semisweet chocolate

Have ready the almonds, chocolate, and a greased baking sheet. In a large skillet combine the sugar, butter, water, and corn syrup and cook the mixture over moderate heat, stirring in one direction only, until the sugar is dissolved. Increase the heat to high and cook the mixture for about 6 minutes more, or until it begins to darken. Quickly stir in the nuts and when the mixture is a deep caramel color pour it onto the baking sheet, spreading it evenly with a spatula. Break the chocolate into pieces on top of the toffee and as it melts spread it evenly over the top. Freeze the toffee on the baking sheet for 1 hour. Break it into pieces while it is still frozen and pack it into a box or tin. The toffee can be stored at room temperature or frozen.

Makes about 1 1/2 pounds.

"Hope" is the thing with feathers – that perches in the soul – and sings the tunes without the words – and never stops – at all –

Emily Dickinson (1830–1886), U.S. poet

Buckeye Candy

1¼ lb. confectioners' sugar
2 sticks butter, melted
1½ tsp. vanilla
8 oz. creamy peanut butter
12 oz. semisweet chocolate morsels

In a bowl mix by hand the sugar, butter, vanilla, and peanut butter until they are well blended and roll the mixture into bite-size balls. Freeze the balls for at least 15 minutes.

While the balls are freezing, melt the chocolate in the top of a double boiler. Using a wooden pick dip the balls in the chocolate, coating them evenly, and return them to the freezer until serving time.

Makes about 4 dozen.

Old-Fashioned Lemon Pecan Bars

1 C. plus 1 tsp. unbleached all-purpose flour
2/3 C. light brown sugar
2 T. grated lemon rind
Pinch of salt
6 T. chilled unsalted butter, cut into pieces
1/4 C. plus 3 T. chopped pecans, toasted
3/4 C. sugar
2 large eggs
1/3 C. lemon juice
1/4 tsp. baking soda
Confectioners' sugar
Pecan halves for garnish

In a food processor mix the cup of flour, brown sugar, half the lemon rind, and the salt and blend in the butter and 1/4 cup pecans, using on and off turns, until the mixture forms coarse crumbs. Press the crumbs firmly into the bottom of a 9-inch-square baking pan and bake the crust on the middle rack of a preheated 350° F. oven for 20 minutes, or until it is golden brown.

In a bowl whisk together the 3/4 cup sugar, eggs, and remaining lemon rind until the mixture is light and fluffy. Whisk in the lemon juice, 1 teaspoon flour, and baking soda and pour the mixture over the crust. Bake the mixture in the preheated oven for 12 minutes, or until the filling is just set and the edges are lightly browned, and transfer it to a rack to cool. Sprinkle the remaining pecans over the filling. Cut the pastry into squares, sift the confectioners' sugar over it, and top each square with a pecan half.

Makes about 25 squares.

Raspberry Chocolate Bars

2 tsp. grated lemon rind
3/4 C. brown sugar
1 C. flour
1 stick unsalted butter
1 tsp. vanilla
1/4 C. seedless raspberry jam
2 oz. bittersweet chocolate, broken into pieces
2 egg whites, at room temperature
1/2 C. almonds
Confectioners' sugar

In a food processor combine the lemon rind, 1/4 cup brown sugar, flour, butter, and vanilla and process the mixture until it resembles coarse crumbs. Press the mixture into a 9-inch-square baking pan and bake it in a preheated 350° F. oven for 15 minutes. Spread it with the jam.

Process the chocolate until it is finely chopped and sprinkle it over the jam. Process the almonds with the remaining brown sugar until they are finely chopped.

In a bowl beat the egg whites until they hold stiff glossy peaks and add them to the almond mixture. Pulse the mixture three times, or until it is just combined, and spread it over the chocolate. Reduce the oven temperature to 325° F. and bake the pastry for 25 minutes, or until the top is lightly browned. Let the pastry cool and sprinkle it with the confectioners' sugar. Cut the pastry into bars.

Makes about 25 bars.

Just as despair can come to one only from other human beings, hope too, can be given to one only by other human beings.

Elie Wiesel (b. 1928),
Rumanian–born U.S. writer

Nanaimo Bars

These bars are a traditional Canadian sweet, which are claimed by many areas of the country, and, accordingly, have numerous variations.

½ C. butter
¼ C. sugar
1 large egg
1 tsp. vanilla
1 T. cocoa
2 C. graham cracker crumbs
1 C. grated coconut
½ C. chopped pecans or walnuts

In a bowl combine the butter, sugar, egg, vanilla, and cocoa and stir the mixture over a pan of boiling water until it is slightly thickened. In a large bowl combine the crumbs, coconut, and nuts and add the butter mixture, combining the mixtures well. Press the mixture evenly into a buttered 9-inch-square baking pan and let it stand for 15 minutes.

Spread Custard Filling over the crumb layer and chill the pan for 15 minutes.

Spread Chocolate Topping over the filling layer and chill the dessert overnight. Cut the dessert into 2-inch squares.

Makes about 16 bars.

Custard Filling

¼ C. butter
2 C. confectioners' sugar
3 T. milk
2 T. powdered custard mix

In a bowl combine the ingredients until the mixture is smooth.

Chocolate Topping

3 oz. semisweet chocolate
1 T. butter

In a small heavy pan melt the chocolate over hot water, being careful not to let it boil. Slowly stir in the butter until the mixture is just blended.

Prune Pecan Squares

2 C. pitted prunes
2 T. orange juice
³/₄ C. chopped pecans
1 C. flour
¹/₂ C. brown sugar
¹/₂ tsp. cinnamon
¹/₄ tsp. salt
1 stick unsalted butter, cut into 8 pieces
¹/₂ tsp. vanilla

In a food processor purée the prunes and orange juice until the mixture is smooth and transfer the purée to a bowl. In the food processor process ¹/₂ cup pecans with the flour, sugar, cinnamon, salt, butter, and vanilla until the mixture resembles coarse crumbs. Reserve ¹/₂ cup of the crumb mixture and press the remaining mixture into a 9-inch-square baking pan. Spread the prune purée on top. Combine the reserved crumb mixture with the remaining pecans and sprinkle the mixture on top. Bake the pastry in a preheated 350° F. oven for 30 minutes, or until the top is golden brown. Let the pastry cool and cut it into squares.

Makes about 16 squares.

Drop small mounds of sweetened whipped cream on a cookie sheet and freeze them. Transfer the mounds to airtight containers and store them in the freezer until needed. They need about fifteen minutes to thaw.

Rhubarb Bars

4 C. chopped fresh or frozen rhubarb
1½ C. sugar
3 T. cornstarch
½ C. water
1 C. butter or margarine, softened
1 C. dark brown sugar
1½ C. flour
½ tsp. baking soda
2 C. old-fashioned oatmeal
⅔ C. chopped pecans or walnuts
1 tsp. vanilla

In a saucepan combine the rhubarb, white sugar, cornstarch, and water, and cook the mixture over moderate heat, stirring occasionally, for 10 to 15 minutes, or until it is thickened.

In an electric mixer bowl combine the butter, brown sugar, flour, baking soda, oatmeal, and nuts and beat the mixture at low speed until it is well combined. Pat two-thirds of the mixture in the bottom of a greased 10- by 15-inch baking dish. Stir the vanilla into the rhubarb mixture and spread the mixture over the crust. Sprinkle the remaining crumb mixture on top and bake the dish in a preheated 350° F. oven for 30 minutes.

Makes twenty-five 2- by 3-inch bars.

Ethereal Almond Cookies

1¾ C. flour
2 tsp. baking powder
¼ tsp. salt
½ C. butter
1 large egg
1 C. sugar
½ tsp. almond extract
½ C. sliced almonds
Milk for brushing
1 C. confectioners' sugar
½ tsp. almond extract
3 to 4 tsp. milk

In a bowl whisk together the flour, baking powder, and salt. In the bowl of an electric mixer cream the butter and beat in the sugar, beating the mixture until it is light. Beat in the egg and almond extract, remove the bowl from the mixer, and stir in the dry ingredients, combining the batter well.

Divide the dough into quarters and form each quarter into a 12-inch roll. Put the rolls on two cookie sheets and flatten them until they are 3 inches wide. Brush the dough with milk and sprinkle it with the almonds. Bake the rolls in a preheated 325° F. oven for 12 to 14 minutes, or until the edges are brown.

While the pastry is still warm cut it diagonally into 1-inch strips and let it cool without separating the strips.

In a small bowl combine the confectioners' sugar, almond extract, and 3 teaspoons milk, stirring until the mixture is smooth and adding just enough milk to make the topping barely liquid. Drizzle the strips with the topping, let the topping solidify, and gently break apart the strips.

Makes about 4 dozen cookies.

Cappuccino Cookies

2 C. flour
1 tsp. cinnamon
1/4 tsp. salt
1/2 C. shortening
1/2 C. butter
1/2 C. sugar
1/2 C. brown sugar
1 T. instant coffee dissolved in 1 tsp. water
2 oz. unsweetened chocolate, melted
1 large egg

In a bowl whisk together the flour, cinnamon, and salt. In the bowl of an electric mixer cream the shortening and butter and add the sugars, beating the mixture until it is light. Beat in the coffee, chocolate, and egg, remove the bowl from the mixer, and stir in the flour mixture, combining the batter well. Chill the batter, covered, for at least 1 hour.

Divide the batter in half, form each half into a 7-inch roll, and chill the rolls, wrapped in plastic wrap, for 6 to 8 hours, or overnight. Cut the rolls into 1/4-inch slices and on baking sheets bake the cookies in a preheated 350° F. oven for 10 to 15 minutes, or until they are almost firm in the center. Let the cookies cool.

Dip half of each cookie in Chocolate Sauce and transfer the cookies to sheets of foil or wax paper. Store the cookies tightly covered.

Makes about 55 cookies.

Chocolate Sauce

1 1/2 C. semisweet chocolate chips
3 T. shortening

In a microwave-safe bowl melt the chocolate chips with the shortening in the microwave, stirring several times, until the mixture is smooth.

In 1717, John Harrison, a New Jersey land agent, purchased 3,000 acres from the Leni Lenape Indians for $50, more than twice the amount paid in 1626 for Manhattan Island. An additional 7,500 acres were added by William Penn, a Pennsylvania landowner, to complete the boundaries of Bernards Township.

Orange Cookies

1 C. shortening
1¾ C. sugar
2 large eggs
4 C. flour
1 tsp. baking powder
1 tsp. baking soda
1 C. milk, left at room temperature for 1
    hour
1 orange, grated and juiced
3 T. butter, melted
Confectioners' sugar

In a large bowl cream the shortening with the sugar and add the eggs, one at a time, beating well after each addition. In another bowl sift together the flour, baking powder, and soda and add the mixture to the sugar mixture alternately with the milk. Reserve 2 tablespoons of the juice and 1 teaspoon of the rind and mix in the remaining orange rind and juice. Drop the batter by teaspoons onto a baking sheet and bake the cookies in a preheated 375° F. oven for 8 to 10 minutes, or until they are lightly golden at the edges.

In a small bowl combine the butter, the reserved juice and rind, and enough confectioners' sugar to thicken the mixture and ice the cookies while they are still warm.

Makes about 6 dozen.

Shortbread Cookies with Warm Apples

⅓ C. ground almonds
¼ C. sugar
2 egg yolks
⅓ C. butter
1 C. bleached flour
Raspberry jam or whipped cream to taste

In a food processor blend the almonds, sugar, and egg yolks, add the butter and flour, and blend the mixture until it just forms a dough. Chill the dough, wrapped in plastic wrap.

Shape the dough into 18 round cookies and on a baking sheet bake the cookies in a preheated 375° F. oven for 10 minutes.

Serve Apple Topping on the warm cookies and top each serving with a dollop of raspberry jam or whipped cream.

Serves 6.

Apple Topping

1 T. butter
4 tart apples, peeled, cored, and sliced
1 T. sugar

In a saucepan melt the butter, add the apples and sugar, and cook the apples for about 10 minutes.

St. George's Shortbread

Packed into decorative tins, these luscious cookies make a sumptuous gift.

> **2 sticks butter, softened**
> **1/2 C. sugar**
> **1/4 C. dark brown sugar**
> **2 T. white cornmeal**
> **1/4 tsp. vanilla**
> **1/2 tsp. salt**
> **1³/4 C. flour**
> **Sugar for sprinkling**

In a mixing bowl cream the butter and sugars. Add the cornmeal, vanilla, and salt and beat in the flour, 1/4 cup at a time. Divide the dough into 4 rounds. Using 2 baking sheets, press each round into a 5-inch circle. With a fork prick each circle to form 8 wedges and press the tines of the fork around the rims to form a decorative edge. Sprinkle the shortbread with sugar and bake it in a preheated 325° F. oven for 20 to 25 minutes, or until it is just firm and still pale. With a knife cut the wedges halfway through along the tine marks and let the shortbread cool completely. Break the shortbread into wedges and store it in an airtight tin container.

Makes 32 wedges.

You can taste and feel, but not describe, the exquisite state of repose produced by tea . . .

Emperor Chien Lung

Yo-Yo's

Also known as Melting Moments, these cookies hail from Australia, where cookies are referred to as "biscuits." They are a truly ethereal fragile cookie – perfect for afternoon tea.

 1½ sticks butter, softened
 ¼ C. confectioners' sugar, sifted
 1 tsp. vanilla
 ¾ C. cornstarch
 1 C. flour

In a bowl cream the butter, sugar, and vanilla until the mixture is fluffy. Into another bowl sift together the cornstarch and flour and stir the mixture into the butter mixture. Spoon the batter into a pastry bag fitted with a large star nozzle and pipe rosettes about 1 inch apart onto lightly greased baking sheets. Bake the cookies in a preheated 350° F. oven for 15 to 20 minutes, or until they are just golden. Let the cookies cool on the baking sheets. Spread the flat sides of half the cookies with Lemon Cream Filling and sandwich them with the remaining cookies.

Lemon Cream Filling

 ½ stick butter, softened
 ⅔ C. confectioners' sugar
 2 tsp. finely grated lemon rind
 1 T. lemon juice

In a bowl beat the butter until it is fluffy, gradually beat in the confectioners' sugar, beating until the mixture is creamy, and stir in the lemon rind and juice.

Makes about 24 cookies.

Heavenly Peach Pie

 3 egg whites
 ½ C. sugar
 14 soda crackers, rolled into fine crumbs
 ¼ tsp. baking powder
 1 tsp. vanilla
 ½ C. chopped pecans
 ⅔ C. heavy cream
 3 T. confectioners' sugar
 ¼ C. shredded coconut, toasted

In the bowl of an electric mixer beat the egg whites until they hold peaks and gradually beat in the sugar, 1 tablespoon at a time, and the vanilla. Continue to beat the meringue at high speed for 2 to 3 minutes more. Fold in the crackers, baking powder, and pecans by hand, scrape the mixture into a 9-inch pie dish, and bake it in a preheated 325° F. oven for 30 minutes. Turn off the oven and leave the crust inside for 15 minutes. Remove the crust and let it cool completely.

Spread the Peach Filling in the crust. In a bowl whip the cream until it holds soft peaks and beat in the confectioners' sugar. Spread the cream mixture over the peaches, swirling it into decorative peaks, and sprinkle the coconut over the top.

Serves 6 to 8.

Peach Filling

 5 ripe peaches, peeled and sliced
 ½ C. sugar

In a bowl combine the peaches with the ½ cup sugar and let them macerate for at least 30 minutes. Drain the juice from the peaches, reserving it for another use.

Pineapple Coconut Pie

1 (9-inch) pie crust, made from Sweet Pastry
    Dough (at right), baked
1 T. cornstarch
1/4 C. cold water
4 egg yolks
1 C. sugar minus 2 T.
1 C. sweetened shredded coconut
2/3 C. light corn syrup
1 C. drained unsweetened crushed
    pineapple
1/2 tsp. ground ginger

In a bowl dissolve the cornstarch in the cold water and whisk in the eggs yolks. In an enameled or stainless steel saucepan combine the sugar, coconut, and corn syrup and heat the mixture over moderate heat until the sugar is dissolved. Stir in the pineapple and ginger and bring the mixture to a boil. Cook the mixture for 1 minute, remove it from the heat, and whisk in the egg yolk mixture, a little at a time, until the filling is well combined. Pour the filling into the shell and bake the pie in a preheated 350° F. oven for 40 to 50 minutes, or until the filling is set. Let the pie cool for at least 30 minutes before serving.

Serves 8.

Sweet Pastry Dough

1 1/4 C. all-purpose flour
2 T. sugar
1/4 tsp. salt
5 T. butter
3 T. solid vegetable shortening
3 T. cold water

In a food processor combine the first 5 ingredients and blend the mixture until it has the consistency of coarse crumbs. Add the water and process the mixture until it just forms a ball. Chill the dough, wrapped in plastic wrap, for at least 30 minutes.

Makes enough dough for one 9- or 10-inch pie or tart.

To Bake Pie or Tart Pastry

Roll out the dough on a well-floured board into a round that is 1 inch larger than the pan on all sides and fit it into the pan. Trim the dough, fold the edges over the rim to make an attractive edge, and crimp the edges. Prick the dough in several places with a fork and chill it for 1 hour.

Gently fit a sheet of foil into the pan, fill it with dried beans or peas or pie weights, and bake the crust in a preheated 425° F. oven for 15 minutes. Remove the foil and weights, reduce the heat to 400° F., and bake the crust for 8 minutes more. (If using dried beans or peas for weights, let them cool and tip them into a storage container. They may be re-used for many years.) Let the crust cool completely on a rack.

Cookbook Committee

Mimi Elder   Kathryn Mustaro
Marilyn Jackson   Pam Smith

Artists

Joy Wallis
Cindy Petterson

Contributors

Beth Adams
Anna Albanese
Cindy Andrews
Candy Anuzis
Carol Barclay
Sandra Barlow
Joan Barnt
Janet Bentley
Betty Bird
Tracey Bredder
Lois Burke
Lynn Campo
MaryBeth Carlucci
Carol Clayton
Lisa Clayton
Casey Collins
Sue Dresner
Lorraine Eloizio
Helen Farhat
Ann Farnham
Martha Feyler

Ann Gratzer
Diane Haley
Karen Hanson
Hannah Harris
Amy Hawk
Janet Hawk
Kathy Henry
Iola Hoffman
Sherry Hoffman
Jan Hoyt
Deb Imperatore
Brooke Jackson
Tim Jackson
Georgine Johnson
Jean Johnson
Cate Kelly
Nadine Lauer-Sinofsky
Bernice Lievense
Ginger Link
Jim Lupia
Roseanne Lynch

Mary Ann Mackey
Greta McElwee
Jan Munch
Claire Payne
Dorothy Petersen
Louise Peterson
Dawna Poyner
Ellyne S. Rabin
Diane Reed
Mary Lou Ricci
Nancy Robinson
Jan Royer
Karen Ryan
Patrice Shapiro
Monica Stephens
Susan Swanson
Maria Tanzola
Elly Todt
Pam Walker
Jean Wallace
Cynthia Wynant

Index

Order Information

A Place at the Table
The Paige Whitney Babies Center
One East Oak Street
Basking Ridge, New Jersey 07920

Please send me _____ copies of *A Place at the Table*   @ $18.95   each $ _____

add postage and handling   @ $ 4.00   each $ _____

Total $ _____

[   ] Check   [   ] American Express   [   ] VISA   Card Number _____

Expiration Date _____   Signature _____

Name _____   Phone _____

Address _____

City _____   State _____   Zip _____

Please make checks payable to The Paige Whitney Babies Center.

- -

A Place at the Table
The Paige Whitney Babies Center
One East Oak Street
Basking Ridge, New Jersey 07920

Please send me _____ copies of *A Place at the Table*   @ $18.95   each $ _____

add postage and handling   @ $ 4.00   each $ _____

Total $ _____

[   ] Check   [   ] American Express   [   ] VISA   Card Number _____

Expiration Date _____   Signature _____

Name _____   Phone _____

Address _____

City _____   State _____   Zip _____

Please make checks payable to The Paige Whitney Babies Center.